Contents

HERSHEY'S

Cookies

Fudgey Coconut Clusters
MAKES ABOUT 2 1/2 DOZEN COOKIES

5 1/3 cups MOUNDS Sweetened Coconut Flakes
1 can (14 oz.) sweetened condensed milk
(not evaporated milk)
2/3 cup HERSHEY'S Cocoa
1/4 cup (1/2 stick) butter, melted
2 teaspoons vanilla extract
1 1/2 teaspoons almond extract
HERSHEY'S Mini KISSES BRAND Milk Chocolates
or candied cherry halves (optional)

1. Heat oven to 350°F. Line cookie sheets with aluminum foil; generously grease foil with vegetable shortening.

2. Combine coconut, sweetened condensed milk, cocoa, melted butter, vanilla and almond extract in large bowl; mix well. Drop by rounded tablespoons onto prepared cookie sheets.

3. Bake 9 to 11 minutes or just until set; press 3 milk chocolates or candied cherry halves in center of each cookie, if desired. Immediately remove cookies to wire rack and cool completely.

VARIATION: Chocolate Chip Macaroons: Omit melted butter and cocoa; stir together other ingredients. Add 1 cup HERSHEY'S Mini Chips Semi-Sweet Chocolate. Bake 9 to 11 minutes or just until set. Immediately remove to wire racks and cool completely.

HERSHEY'S

The Tradition
Continues

We at HERSHEY'S Kitchens have always been proud that our products are used by so many people in so many different ways. We are thrilled to be part of the imaginative recipes people create when baking for family and friends. Our commitment to supporting the imagination and creativity of chocolate lovers everywhere goes all the way back to Milton S. Hershey, the founder of our company and creator of our original products. A great entrepreneur and philanthropist, Mr. Hershey measured success, not in dollars, but in terms of a good product to pass on to the public.

Milton S. Hershey was born in 1857 near Derry Church, Pennsylvania, and began his confectionery career as an apprentice to a candy maker in Lancaster, Pennsylvania. After struggling to establish a successful company in various locations across the nation, he returned to Lancaster in 1886 to found the business that established his candy-making reputation, the Lancaster Caramel Company.

In 1893, Mr. Hershey became fascinated with German chocolate making machinery on exhibit at the World's Columbian Exposition in Chicago and purchased the equipment and had it installed in his Lancaster plant. He soon began producing his own chocolate coatings for caramels, and in 1894 the Hershey Chocolate Company was born as a subsidiary of his Lancaster caramel business. In addition to chocolate coating, Mr. Hershey produced breakfast cocoa, sweet chocolate, and baking chocolate. After selling his caramel business to concentrate on chocolate, Mr. Hershey returned to his birthplace and began construction in 1903 on what is now the world's largest chocolate manufacturing plant, located in a town now known as Hershey, Pennsylvania.

Mr. Hershey later used his fortune primarily for two projects: the town of Hershey and the Hershey Industrial School, now known as the Milton Hershey School. Saddened because

they had no children of their own, Milton and Catherine Hershey founded this school for orphaned boys on November 15, 1909. The school still serves as the opportunity of a lifetime for children in financial and social need from all over America.

Located in Hershey, Pennsylvania, the residential school provides a pre-K through 12th grade education and a caring, family-like home setting—free of charge—to children in financial need. The Milton Hershey School has been helping children from low-income families for more than 95 years. Milton Hershey saw the school as his greatest accomplishment. However, Hershey is best known for quality milk chocolate products.

One of the initial three products Milton Hershey introduced in 1894 is HERSHEY'S Cocoa, a natural source of flavanol antioxidants. It is still a staple in kitchens across America. But this versatile product isn't just for baking anymore. HERSHEY'S Cocoa can add a fun and flavorful new kick to a variety of foods, from meats to delicate fish— even risotto and chili.

The cocoa tradition continues with the launch of HERSHEY'S SPECIAL DARK® Cocoa, which is specially blended to deliver a darker, richer flavor for more sophisticated desserts.

Since the 1920s, HERSHEY'S Kitchens have created mouthwatering recipes for spectacular cakes, irresistible cookies, and much more. These recipes featuring Hershey's ingredients are easy to prepare and create smiles at every family function.

HERSHEY'S 3 Books in 1 includes many classic favorites you will treasure for years to come. When your family and friends taste our recipes, we're sure they'll agree that HERSHEY'S baking products make mealtimes sweeter.

HERSHEY'S®
Sweet Treats

Reduced-Sugar Chocolate Chocolate Chip Cookies

MAKES 3 DOZEN COOKIES

½ cup (1 stick) butter or margarine, softened

¼ cup sugar

½ cup measure-for-measure sugar substitute

1 egg

1 teaspoon vanilla extract

1 cup all-purpose flour

3 tablespoons HERSHEY'S Cocoa or HERSHEY'S SPECIAL DARK Cocoa

½ teaspoon baking soda

⅛ teaspoon salt

2 tablespoons skim milk

⅓ cup HERSHEY'S Mini Chips Semi-Sweet Chocolate

1. Heat oven to 375°F.

2. Beat butter, sugar and sugar substitute with electric mixer on medium speed in medium bowl until well blended. Add egg and vanilla; beat well. Stir together flour, cocoa, baking soda and salt; add alternately with milk to butter mixture, beating until well blended. Stir in small chocolate chips. Drop by teaspoons onto ungreased cookie sheet.

3. Bake 7 to 9 minutes or just until set. Remove to wire rack and cool completely.

Chewy Drizzled Cinnamon Chip Cookies

MAKES ABOUT 5 DOZEN COOKIES

¾ cup (1½ sticks) butter or margarine, softened
1 cup packed light brown sugar
¼ cup light corn syrup
1 egg
1⅔ cups (10-oz. pkg.) HERSHEY'S Cinnamon Chips, divided
2½ cups all-purpose flour
2 teaspoons baking soda
¼ teaspoon salt
1 cup finely ground pecans or walnuts
1½ teaspoons shortening

1. Beat butter and brown sugar with electric mixer on medium speed in large bowl until fluffy. Add corn syrup and egg; mix well.

2. Place 1 cup cinnamon chips in microwave-safe bowl. Microwave at MEDIUM (50%) 1 minute; stir. If necessary, microwave at MEDIUM an additional 15 seconds at a time, stirring after each heating, just until chips are melted when stirred. Stir melted chips into butter mixture.

3. Stir together flour, baking soda and salt; add to cinnamon chips mixture, beating with electric mixer just until blended. Cover; refrigerate dough about 1 hour or until firm enough to handle.

4. Heat oven to 350°F. Shape dough into 1-inch balls; roll in nuts, lightly pressing nuts into dough. Place on ungreased cookie sheets.

5. Bake 8 to 10 minutes or until golden around edges. Cool slightly. Remove to wire rack and cool completely.

6. Place remaining ⅔ cup cinnamon chips and shortening (do not use butter, margarine, spread or oil) in small microwave-safe bowl. Microwave at MEDIUM (50%) 1 minute or until chips are melted and mixture is smooth when stirred. Drizzle evenly over cooled cookies.

HERSHEY'S Double Chocolate Mint Cookies

MAKES ABOUT 2 1/2 DOZEN COOKIES

⅔ cup butter or margarine, softened

1 cup sugar

1 egg

1 teaspoon vanilla extract

1 cup all-purpose flour

½ cup HERSHEY'S Cocoa

½ teaspoon baking soda

¼ teaspoon salt

1⅔ cups (10-oz. pkg.) HERSHEY'S Mint Chocolate Chips

1. Heat oven to 350°F.

2. Beat butter and sugar with electric mixer on medium speed in large bowl until creamy. Add egg and vanilla; beat well. Stir together flour, cocoa, baking soda and salt; gradually add to butter mixture, beating well. Stir in mint chocolate chips. Drop by rounded teaspoons onto ungreased cookie sheet.

3. Bake 8 to 9 minutes or just until set; do not overbake. Cool slightly. Remove to wire rack and cool completely.

Peanut Butter and Milk Chocolate Chip Tassies

MAKES 3 DOZEN COOKIES

- ¾ cup (1½ sticks) butter, softened
- 1 package (3 oz.) cream cheese, softened
- 1½ cups all-purpose flour
- ¾ cup sugar, divided
- 1 egg, slightly beaten
- 2 tablespoons butter or margarine, melted
- ¼ teaspoon lemon juice
- ¼ teaspoon vanilla extract
- 1 cup HERSHEY'S Milk Chocolate Chips
- 1 cup REESE'S Peanut Butter Chips
- 2 teaspoons shortening (do not use butter, margarine, spread or oil)

1. Beat butter and cream cheese with electric mixer on medium speed in medium bowl until creamy. Add flour and ¼ cup sugar and beat until well blended. Cover; refrigerate about one hour or until dough is firm. Shape dough into 1-inch balls; press each ball onto bottom and up sides of about 36 small muffin cups (1¾ inches in diameter).

2. Heat oven to 350°F. Combine egg, remaining ½ cup sugar, melted butter, lemon juice and vanilla in small bowl; stir until smooth. Stir together milk chocolate chips and peanut butter chips. Set aside ⅓ cup chip mixture; add remainder to egg mixture. Evenly fill muffin cups with egg mixture.

3. Bake 20 to 25 minutes or until filling is set and lightly browned. Cool completely; remove to wire rack.

4. Combine reserved ⅓ cup chip mixture and shortening in small microwave-safe bowl. Microwave at MEDIUM (50%) 30 seconds; stir. If necessary, microwave at MEDIUM an additional 10 seconds at a time, stirring after each heating, until chips are melted and mixture is smooth when stirred. Drizzle over tops of tassies.

Buche De Noel Cookies

MAKES ABOUT 2½ DOZEN COOKIES

- ⅔ cup butter or margarine, softened
- 1 cup granulated sugar
- 2 eggs
- 2 teaspoons vanilla extract
- 2½ cups all-purpose flour
- ½ cup HERSHEY'S Cocoa
- ½ teaspoon baking soda
- ¼ teaspoon salt
  Mocha Frosting (recipe follows)
  Powdered sugar (optional)

1. Beat butter and sugar with electric mixer on medium speed in large bowl until well blended. Add eggs and vanilla; beat until fluffy. Stir together flour, cocoa, baking soda and salt; gradually add to butter mixture, beating until well blended. Cover; refrigerate dough 1 to 2 hours.

2. Heat oven to 350°F. Shape heaping teaspoons of dough into logs about 2½ inches long and ¾ inches in diameter; place on ungreased cookie sheets. Bake 7 to 9 minutes or until set. Cool slightly. Remove to wire rack and cool completely.

3. Frost cookies with Mocha Frosting. Using tines of fork, draw lines through frosting to imitate tree bark. Lightly dust with powdered sugar, if desired.

MOCHA FROSTING

MAKES ABOUT 1⅔ CUPS FROSTING

- 6 tablespoons butter or margarine, softened
- 2⅔ cups powdered sugar
- ⅓ cup HERSHEY'S Cocoa
- 3 to 4 tablespoons milk

2 teaspoons powdered instant espresso dissolved in
   1 teaspoon hot water

1 teaspoon vanilla extract

Beat butter in medium bowl. Add powdered sugar and cocoa
alternately with milk, dissolved espresso and vanilla, beating
to spreadable consistency.

Mixed Chocolate Chip Cookies

MAKES ABOUT 3 1/2 DOZEN COOKIES

 6 tablespoons butter, softened
 1/3 cup butter flavored shortening
 1/2 cup packed light brown sugar
 1/3 cup granulated sugar
 1 egg
 1 1/2 teaspoons vanilla extract
 1 1/4 cups all-purpose flour
 1/2 teaspoon baking soda
 1/2 teaspoon salt
 2 cups (12-oz. pkg.) HERSHEY'S SPECIAL DARK
   Chocolate Chips or HERSHEY'S Semi-Sweet
   Chocolate Chips
 1 cup HERSHEY'S Milk Chocolate Chips
 3/4 cup chopped nuts (optional)

1. Heat oven to 350°F.

2. Beat butter and shortening with electric mixer in large bowl until well blended. Add brown sugar and granulated sugar; beat thoroughly. Add egg and vanilla, beating until well blended. Stir together flour, baking soda and salt; gradually beat into butter mixture. Stir in chocolate chips and nuts, if desired. Drop by rounded teaspoons onto ungreased cookie sheet.

3. Bake 10 to 12 minutes or until lightly browned. Cool slightly. Remove to wire rack and cool completely.

Chewy Coconut Oatmeal Drops

MAKES ABOUT 5 DOZEN COOKIES

- ¾ cup (1½ sticks) butter or margarine, softened
- ¾ cup granulated sugar
- ¾ cup packed light brown sugar
- 2 eggs
- 1 teaspoon vanilla extract
- 2 cups all-purpose flour
- 1 teaspoon baking soda
- ½ teaspoon salt
- 2 cups MOUNDS Sweetened Coconut Flakes
- 1½ cups quick-cooking or regular rolled oats

1. Heat oven to 350°F.

2. Beat butter, granulated sugar and brown sugar with electric mixer on medium speed in large bowl until well blended. Beat in eggs and vanilla. Stir together flour, baking soda and salt; add to butter mixture, beating until blended. Stir in coconut and oats (dough will be thick).

3. Drop by teaspoons onto ungreased cookie sheet. Bake 8 to 10 minutes or until edges are lightly browned. Cool slightly. Remove to wire rack and cool completely.

Holiday Double Peanut Butter Fudge Cookies

MAKES ABOUT 3 1/2 DOZEN COOKIES

1   can (14 oz.) sweetened condensed milk
    (not evaporated milk)
¾   cup REESE'S Creamy Peanut Butter
2   cups all-purpose biscuit baking mix
1   teaspoon vanilla extract
¾   cup REESE'S Peanut Butter Chips
¼   cup granulated sugar
½   teaspoon red colored sugar
½   teaspoon green colored sugar

1. Heat oven to 375°F.

2. Beat sweetened condensed milk and peanut butter with electric mixer on medium speed in large bowl until smooth. Beat in baking mix and vanilla; stir in peanut butter chips. Set aside.

3. Stir together granulated sugar and colored sugars in small bowl. Shape dough into 1-inch balls; roll in sugar. Place 2 inches apart on ungreased cookie sheets; flatten slightly with bottom of glass.

4. Bake 6 to 8 minutes or until very lightly browned (do not overbake). Cool slightly. Remove to wire rack and cool completely. Store in tightly covered container.

Oatmeal Butterscotch Cookies

MAKES ABOUT 4 DOZEN COOKIES

¾ cup (1½ sticks) butter or margarine, softened
¾ cup granulated sugar
¾ cup packed light brown sugar
2 eggs
1 teaspoon vanilla extract
1¼ cups all-purpose flour
1 teaspoon baking soda
½ teaspoon ground cinnamon
½ teaspoon salt
3 cups quick-cooking or regular rolled oats
1¾ cups (11-oz. pkg.) HERSHEY'S Butterscotch Chips

1. Heat oven to 375°F.

2. Beat butter, granulated sugar and brown sugar with electric mixer on medium speed in large bowl until well blended. Add eggs and vanilla; beat well. Stir together flour, baking soda, cinnamon and salt; gradually add to butter mixture, beating until well blended. Stir in oats and butterscotch chips; mix well. Drop by heaping teaspoons onto ungreased cookie sheet.

3. Bake 8 to 10 minutes or until golden brown. Cool slightly. Remove to wire rack and cool completely.

Lemon Coconut Pixies

MAKES ABOUT 4 DOZEN COOKIES

¼ cup (½ stick) butter or margarine, softened
1 cup granulated sugar
2 eggs
1½ teaspoons freshly grated lemon peel
1½ cups all-purpose flour
2 teaspoons baking powder
¼ teaspoon salt
1 cup MOUNDS Sweetened Coconut Flakes
Powdered sugar

1. Heat oven to 300°F.

2. Beat butter, granulated sugar, eggs and lemon peel in large bowl until well blended. Stir together flour, baking powder and salt; gradually add to lemon mixture, beating until blended. Stir in coconut. Cover; refrigerate dough about 1 hour or until firm enough to handle. Shape into 1-inch balls; roll in powdered sugar. Place 2 inches apart on ungreased cookie sheet.

3. Bake 15 to 18 minutes or until edges are set. Immediately remove from cookie sheet to wire rack. Cool completely. Store in tightly covered container in cool, dry place.

Really Chocolate Chocolate Chip Cookies

MAKES ABOUT 5 DOZEN COOKIES

6 tablespoons butter or margarine, softened
6 tablespoons butter flavored shortening
⅔ cup packed light brown sugar
½ cup granulated sugar
2 eggs
2 tablespoons milk
2 teaspoons vanilla extract
1 cup all-purpose flour
½ cup HERSHEY'S Cocoa
½ teaspoon baking soda
½ teaspoon salt
2 cups (12-oz pkg.) HERSHEY'S SPECIAL DARK Chocolate Chips
1 cup chopped nuts
Powdered sugar (optional)

1. Heat oven to 350°F.

2. Beat butter and shortening with electric mixer on medium speed in large bowl until well blended. Add brown sugar and granulated sugar and beat well. Add egg, milk and vanilla, and beat until well blended.

3. Stir together flour, cocoa, baking soda and salt; beat into butter mixture. Stir in chocolate chips and nuts. Drop by teaspoons onto ungreased cookie sheets.

4. Bake 10 to 12 minutes or until edges are set. Cool slightly. Remove to wire rack and cool completely. Sprinkle with powdered sugar, if desired.

HERSHEY'S
BAKING &
Confection

KISSES Fluted Cups
with Peanut Butter Filling
MAKES ABOUT 2 DOZEN PIECES

72 HERSHEY'S KISSES BRAND Milk Chocolates, divided
 1 cup REESE'S Creamy Peanut Butter
 1 cup powdered sugar
 1 tablespoon butter or margarine, softened

1. Line small baking cups (1¾ inches in diameter) with small paper baking liners. Remove wrappers from chocolates.

2. Place 48 chocolates in small microwave-safe bowl. Microwave at MEDIUM (50%) 1 minute; stir. Microwave at MEDIUM an additional 10 seconds at a time, stirring after each heating, just until chocolate is melted when stirred. Using small brush, coat inside of paper cups with melted chocolate.

3. Refrigerate 20 minutes; reapply melted chocolate to any thin spots. Refrigerate until firm, preferably overnight. Gently peel paper from chocolate cups.

4. Beat peanut butter, powdered sugar and butter with electric mixer on medium speed in small bowl until smooth. Spoon into chocolate cups. Before serving, top each cup with a chocolate piece. Cover; store cups in refrigerator.

HERSHEY'S Triple Chocolate Cookies

MAKES ABOUT 4 DOZEN COOKIES

48 HERSHEY'S KISSES_{BRAND} Milk Chocolates or HERSHEY'S KISSES_{BRAND} Milk Chocolates with Almonds

½ cup (1 stick) butter or margarine, softened

¾ cup granulated sugar

¾ cup packed light brown sugar

1 teaspoon vanilla extract

2 eggs

1 tablespoon milk

2¼ cups all-purpose flour

⅓ cup HERSHEY'S Cocoa

1 teaspoon baking soda

½ teaspoon salt

1 cup HERSHEY'S SPECIAL DARK Chocolate Chips or HERSHEY'S Semi-Sweet Chocolate Chips

1. Remove wrappers from chocolates. Heat oven to 350°F.

2. Beat butter, granulated sugar, brown sugar and vanilla with electric mixer on medium speed in large bowl until well blended. Add eggs and milk; beat well.

3. Stir together flour, cocoa, baking soda and salt; gradually beat into butter mixture, beating until well blended. Stir in chocolate chips. Shape dough into 1-inch balls. Place on ungreased cookie sheet.

4. Bake 10 to 11 minutes or until set. Gently press a chocolate into center of each cookie; remove from cookie sheet to wire rack. Cool completely.

VARIATION: For vanilla cookies, omit cocoa and add an additional ⅓ cup all-purpose flour.

Secret KISSES Cookies

MAKES 3 DOZEN COOKIES

- 1 cup (2 sticks) butter or margarine, softened
- ½ cup granulated sugar
- 1 teaspoon vanilla extract
- 1¾ cups all-purpose flour
- 1 cup finely chopped walnuts or almonds
- 36 HERSHEY'S KISSES BRAND Milk Chocolates or HERSHEY'S KISSES BRAND Milk Chocolates with Almonds
- Powdered sugar

1. Beat butter, granulated sugar and vanilla with electric mixer on medium speed in large bowl until fluffy. Add flour and walnuts; mix on low speed until well blended. Cover; refrigerate 1 to 2 hours or until dough is firm enough to handle.

2. Remove wrappers from chocolates. Heat oven to 375°F. Using about 1 tablespoon dough for each cookie, shape dough around each chocolate; roll into smooth balls. (Be sure to cover each chocolate piece completely.) Place on ungreased cookie sheets.

3. Bake 10 to 12 minutes or until cookies are set but not browned. Cool slightly; remove to wire rack. While still slightly warm, roll in powdered sugar. Cool completely. Store in tightly covered container. Roll again in powdered sugar just before serving.

VARIATION: Sift together 1 tablespoon HERSHEY'S Cocoa with ⅓ cup powdered sugar. After removing cookies from oven roll in cocoa mixture instead of powdered sugar.

KISSES Chocolate Mousse

MAKES 4 SERVINGS

36 HERSHEY'S KISSES BRAND Milk Chocolates

1½ cups miniature or 15 regular marshmallows

⅓ cup milk

2 teaspoons kirsch (cherry brandy) or ¼ teaspoon almond extract

6 to 8 drops red food color (optional)

1 cup cold whipping cream
Additional HERSHEY'S KISSES BRAND Milk Chocolates (optional)

1. Remove wrappers from chocolates. Combine marshmallows and milk in small saucepan. Cook over low heat, stirring constantly, until marshmallows are melted and mixture is smooth. Remove from heat.

2. Pour ⅓ cup marshmallow mixture into medium bowl; stir in brandy and food color, if desired. Set aside. To remaining marshmallow mixture, add 36 chocolates; return to low heat, stirring constantly until chocolate is melted. Remove from heat; cool to room temperature.

3. Beat whipping cream in small bowl until stiff. Fold 1 cup whipped cream into chocolate mixture. Gradually fold remaining whipped cream into reserved mixture. Fill 4 parfait glasses about ¾ full with chocolate mousse; spoon or pipe reserved marshmallow mixture on top. Refrigerate 3 to 4 hours or until set. Garnish with additional chocolates, if desired.

KISSES Macaroon Cookies

MAKES ABOUT 4 DOZEN COOKIES

⅓ cup butter or margarine, softened
1 package (3 oz.) cream cheese, softened
¾ cup sugar
1 egg yolk
2 teaspoons almond extract
2 teaspoons orange juice
1¼ cups all-purpose flour
2 teaspoons baking powder
¼ teaspoon salt
5 cups MOUNDS Sweetened Coconut Flakes, divided
48 HERSHEY'S KISSES BRAND Milk Chocolates

1. Beat butter, cream cheese and sugar with electric mixer on medium speed in large bowl until well blended. Add egg yolk, almond extract and orange juice; beat well. Stir together flour, baking powder and salt; gradually add to butter mixture, beating until well blended. Stir in 3 cups coconut.

2. Cover; refrigerate 1 hour or until firm enough to handle. Remove wrappers from chocolates. Heat oven to 350°F. Shape dough into 1-inch balls; roll balls in remaining 2 cups coconut. Place on ungreased cookie sheet.

3. Bake 10 to 12 minutes or until lightly browned. Remove from oven; immediately press chocolate on top of each cookie. Cool 1 minute; carefully remove from cookie sheet to wire rack. Cool completely.

KISSES Chocolate Chip Cookies

MAKES 4 DOZEN COOKIES

48 HERSHEY'S KISSES BRAND Milk Chocolates or HERSHEY'S KISSES BRAND Milk Chocolates with Almonds
1 cup (2 sticks) butter or margarine, softened
⅓ cup granulated sugar
⅓ cup packed light brown sugar
1 teaspoon vanilla extract
2 cups all-purpose flour
1¼ cups HERSHEY'S Mini Chips Semi-Sweet Chocolate, divided
1 teaspoon shortening

1. Heat oven to 375°F. Remove wrappers from chocolates.

2. Beat butter, granulated sugar, brown sugar and vanilla with electric mixer on medium speed in large bowl until well blended. Add flour to butter mixture; beat until smooth. Stir in 1 cup mini chocolate chips. Mold scant tablespoon dough around each milk chocolate piece, covering chocolates completely. Shape into balls; place 2 inches apart on ungreased cookie sheets.

3. Bake 10 to 12 minutes or until set. Cool slightly. Remove to wire rack and cool completely. Place remaining ¼ cup mini chocolate chips and shortening in small microwave-safe bowl. Microwave at MEDIUM (50%) 30 seconds; stir. If necessary, microwave at MEDIUM an additional 10 seconds at a time, stirring after each heating, until chocolate is melted and smooth when stirred. Drizzle over cookies.

Peanut Butter Blossoms
MAKES ABOUT 4 DOZEN COOKIES

- 48 HERSHEY'S KISSES BRAND Milk Chocolates
- ½ cup shortening
- ¾ cup REESE'S Creamy Peanut Butter
- ⅓ cup granulated sugar
- ⅓ cup packed light brown sugar
- 1 egg
- 2 tablespoons milk
- 1 teaspoon vanilla extract
- 1½ cups all-purpose flour
- 1 teaspoon baking soda
- ½ teaspoon salt
- Granulated sugar

1. Heat oven to 375°F. Remove wrappers from chocolates.

2. Beat shortening and peanut butter with electric mixer on medium speed in large bowl until well blended. Add ⅓ cup granulated sugar and brown sugar; beat until fluffy. Add egg, milk and vanilla; beat well. Stir together flour, baking soda and salt; gradually beat into peanut butter mixture.

3. Shape dough into 1-inch balls. Roll in granulated sugar; place on ungreased cookie sheet.

4. Bake 8 to 10 minutes or until lightly browned. Immediately press 1 chocolate into center of each cookie (cookies will crack around edges), then remove to wire rack. Cool completely.

HERSHEY'S KISSES Birthday Cake

MAKES 10 TO 12 SERVINGS

- 2 cups sugar
- 1¾ cups all-purpose flour
- ¾ cup HERSHEY'S Cocoa or HERSHEY'S SPECIAL DARK Cocoa
- 1½ teaspoons baking powder
- 1½ teaspoons baking soda
- 1 teaspoon salt
- 2 eggs
- 1 cup milk
- ½ cup vegetable oil
- 2 teaspoons vanilla extract
- 1 cup boiling water
  Vanilla Buttercream Frosting (recipe follows)
  HERSHEY'S KISSES BRAND Milk Chocolates

1. Heat oven to 350°F. Grease and flour two 9-inch round baking pans or one 13×9×2-inch baking pan.

2. Stir together sugar, flour, cocoa, baking powder, baking soda and salt in large bowl. Add eggs, milk, oil and vanilla; beat with electric mixer on medium speed for 2 minutes. Stir in boiling water (batter will be thin). Pour batter into prepared pans.

3. Bake 30 to 35 minutes for round pans, 35 to 40 minutes for rectangular pan or until wooden pick inserted in center comes out clean. Cool 10 minutes; turn out onto wire racks. Cool completely.

4. Frost with Vanilla Buttercream Frosting. Remove wrappers from chocolates. Garnish top and sides of cake with chocolates.

VANILLA BUTTERCREAM FROSTING

MAKES ABOUT 2 1/3 CUPS FROSTING

- 1/3 cup butter or margarine, softened
- 4 cups powdered sugar, divided
- 3 to 4 tablespoons milk
- 1 1/2 teaspoons vanilla extract

Beat butter with electric mixer on medium speed in large bowl until creamy. With mixer running, gradually add about 2 cups powdered sugar, beating until well combined. Slowly beat in milk and vanilla. Gradually add remaining powdered sugar, beating until smooth. Add additional milk, if necessary, until frosting is desired consistency.

KISSES Christmas Candies

MAKES ABOUT 14 CANDIES

About 14 HERSHEY'S KISSESBRAND **Milk Chocolates**

¾ **cup ground almonds**
⅓ **cup powdered sugar**
1 **tablespoon light corn syrup**
½ **teaspoon almond extract**
   Few drops green food color
   Few drops red food color
   Granulated sugar

1. Remove wrappers from chocolates. Stir together ground almonds and powdered sugar in medium bowl until well combined. Stir together corn syrup and almond extract; pour over almond mixture, stirring until completely blended. Divide mixture between two bowls.

2. Stir green food color into one bowl; with clean hands, mix until color is well blended and mixture clings together. Repeat with red food color and half ground almond mixture.

3. Shape at least 1 teaspoon almond mixture around each chocolate. Roll in granulated sugar.

HUGS & KISSES Crescents

MAKES 8 CRESCENTS

1 package (8 oz.) refrigerated crescent dinner rolls
24 HERSHEY'S KISSES ᴮᴿᴬᴺᴰ Milk Chocolates or HERSHEY'S
     HUGS ᴮᴿᴬᴺᴰ Chocolates
    Powdered sugar

1. Heat oven to 375°F. Separate dough into 8 triangles. Remove wrappers from chocolates.

2. Place 3 chocolates at center of wide end of each triangle; chocolates on each piece of dough should be touching one another. Starting at wide end, roll to opposite point; pinch edges to seal. Place rolls, pointed side down, on ungreased cookie sheet. Curve into crescent shape.

3. Bake 10 minutes or until lightly browned. Cool slightly; sift with powdered sugar. Serve warm.

NOTE: Leftover crescents can be reheated in microwave for a few seconds.

Chocolate Lover's Ice Cream Sauce

MAKES ABOUT 1 CUP SAUCE

30 HERSHEY'S KISSES BRAND Milk Chocolates
½ cup HERSHEY'S Chocolate Syrup
   Any flavor ice cream
   Sweetened whipped cream
   Additional HERSHEY'S KISSES BRAND Milk Chocolates,
      if desired

1. Remove wrappers from chocolates. Combine syrup and chocolates in small heavy saucepan. Cook over very low heat, stirring constantly, until chocolates are melted and mixture is smooth; remove from heat.

2. Spoon sauce over scoops of ice cream. Garnish with sweetened whipped cream and additional chocolates. Serve immediately. Cover and refrigerate leftover sauce.

To reheat, place small bowl containing sauce in larger bowl containing about 1 inch very hot water. Allow to stand a few minutes to soften. Stir to desired consistency.

MICROWAVE DIRECTIONS: Combine syrup and chocolates in small microwave-safe bowl. Microwave at MEDIUM (50%) 15 seconds; stir well. Microwave at MEDIUM 30 seconds or until chocolates are melted and mixture is smooth when stirred. To reheat refrigerated sauce, microwave at MEDIUM a few seconds at a time until of desired consistency.

KISSES Candy Twists

 MAKES ABOUT 36 PIECES

1   bag small pretzels (twisted)

HERSHEY'S KISSES BRAND Milk Chocolates

Decorative garnishes such as: REESE'S PIECES Candies, silver dragées, small holiday themed candies, nut pieces, miniature marshmallows, candied cherry pieces

1. Heat oven to 350°F. Remove wrappers from chocolates.

2. Place pretzels on ungreased cookie sheet. Place 1 unwrapped chocolate on top of each pretzel.

3. Bake 2 to 3 minutes or until the chocolate is soft, but not melted.

4. Remove from oven; gently press decorative garnish on top of softened chocolate piece. Cool.

HERSHEY'S

REESE'S Peanut Butter & HERSHEY'S KISSES Chocolate Pie

MAKES 8 SERVINGS

About 42 HERSHEY'S KISSES BRAND Milk Chocolates, divided
2 tablespoons milk
1 packaged (8-inch) crumb crust (6 oz.)
1 package (8 oz.) cream cheese, softened
¾ cup sugar
1 cup REESE'S Creamy Peanut Butter
1 tub (8 oz.) frozen non-dairy whipped topping, thawed and divided

1. Remove wrappers from chocolates. Place 26 chocolates and milk in small microwave-safe bowl. Microwave at MEDIUM (50%) 1 minute or just until melted and smooth when stirred. Spread evenly on bottom of crust. Refrigerate about ½ hour.

2. Beat cream cheese with electric mixer on medium speed in medium bowl until smooth; gradually beat in sugar, then peanut butter, beating well after each addition. Reserve ½ cup whipped topping; fold remaining whipped topping into peanut butter mixture. Spoon into crust over chocolate. Cover; refrigerate about 6 hours or until set.

3. Garnish with reserved whipped topping and remaining chocolate. Cover; refrigerate leftover pie.

KISSES Cocoa Cookies

MAKES ABOUT 4 1/2 DOZEN COOKIES

1 cup (2 sticks) butter or margarine, softened
2/3 cup sugar
1 teaspoon vanilla extract
1 2/3 cups all-purpose flour
1/4 cup HERSHEY'S Cocoa
1 cup finely chopped pecans
   About 54 HERSHEY'S KISSES BRAND Milk Chocolates
   Powdered sugar

1. Beat butter, sugar and vanilla with electric mixer on medium speed in large bowl until creamy. Stir together flour and cocoa. Gradually beat into butter mixture, mixing until blended. Add pecans; beat until well blended. Refrigerate dough about 1 hour or until firm enough to handle.

2. Heat oven to 375°F. Remove wrappers from chocolates. Mold scant tablespoon of dough around each chocolate, covering completely. Shape into balls. Place on ungreased cookie sheet.

3. Bake 10 to 12 minutes or until set. Cool about 1 minute; remove from cookie sheet to wire rack. Cool completely. Roll in powdered sugar. Roll in sugar again just before serving, if desired.

KISSES Sweetheart Cookies

YIELD WILL VARY ACCORDING
TO COOKIE RECIPE USED

Sugar Cookie Dough (purchased or your favorite recipe)
HERSHEY'S Cocoa
48 **HERSHEY'S KISSES**BRAND **Milk Chocolates, unwrapped***
1 **teaspoon shortening (do not use butter, margarine, spread or oil)**

**Forty-eight KISSES*BRAND *Milk Chocolates is enough to garnish about 3 dozen cookies following these directions, adjust as necessary for sugar cookie recipe.*

1. Heat oven to as directed for sugar cookies. Divide dough in half; roll out one half at a time to ¼-inch thickness following package or recipe directions. Cut out with 2-inch heart shaped cookie cutters; place on ungreased cookie sheet.

2. Bake according to package or recipe directions. Cool completely on cooling racks. Sprinkle cookies with cocoa.

3. Place 12 chocolates and shortening in small microwave-safe bowl. Microwave at MEDIUM (50%) 1 minute; stir. If necessary, microwave at MEDIUM 15 seconds at a time, stirring after each heating, until chocolates are melted and mixture is smooth when stirred. Drizzle onto cookies. Before drizzle sets, place 1 chocolate in center of each heart.

HERSHEY'S Chocolate Peppermint Roll

MAKES 10 TO 12 SERVINGS

CHOCOLATE SPONGE ROLL

- 4 eggs, separated
- ½ cup plus ⅓ cup sugar, divided
- 1 teaspoon vanilla extract
- ½ cup all-purpose flour
- ⅓ cup HERSHEY'S Cocoa
- ½ teaspoon baking powder
- ¼ teaspoon baking soda
- ⅛ teaspoon salt
- ⅓ cup water

PEPPERMINT FILLING

- 1 cup whipping cream, cold
- ¼ cup powdered sugar
- ¼ cup finely crushed hard peppermint candy
  or ½ teaspoon mint extract and a few drops
  red food color

CHOCOLATE GLAZE

- 2 tablespoons butter or margarine
- 2 tablespoons HERSHEY'S Cocoa
- 2 tablespoons water
- 1 cup powdered sugar
- ½ teaspoon vanilla extract

(recipe continued on page 44)

LUSCIOUS HOLIDAY DESSERTS

HERSHEY'S

(recipe continued from page 42)

1. For Chocolate Sponge Roll, heat oven to 375°F. Line 15½×10½×1-inch jelly-roll pan with foil; generously grease foil.

2. Beat egg whites with electric mixer on high speed in large bowl until soft peaks form; gradually add ½ cup sugar, beating until stiff peaks form. Set aside.

3. Beat egg yolks and vanilla with electric mixer on medium speed in medium bowl 3 minutes. Gradually add remaining ⅓ cup sugar; continue beating 2 additional minutes. Stir together flour, cocoa, baking powder, baking soda and salt. With mixer on low speed, add flour mixture to egg yolk mixture alternately with water, beating just until batter is smooth. Using rubber spatula, gradually fold beaten egg whites into chocolate mixture until well blended. Spread batter evenly in prepared pan.

4. Bake 12 to 15 minutes or until top springs back when touched lightly. Immediately loosen cake from edges of pan; invert onto clean towel sprinkled with powdered sugar. Carefully peel off foil. Immediately roll cake in towel, starting from narrow end; place on wire rack to cool completely.

5. For Peppermint Filling, beat whipping cream with electric mixer on medium speed in medium bowl until slightly thickened. Add powdered sugar and peppermint candy or mint extract and food color, if desired; beat cream until stiff peaks form.

6. For Chocolate Glaze, melt butter in small saucepan over very low heat; add cocoa and water, stirring until smooth and slightly thickened. Remove from heat and cool slightly. (Cool completely for thicker frosting.) Gradually beat in powdered sugar and vanilla extract.

7. Carefully unroll cake; remove towel. Spread cake with Peppermint Filling; reroll cake. Glaze with Chocolate Glaze. Refrigerate until just before serving. Cover; refrigerate leftover dessert.

VARIATION: Substitute Coffee Filling for Peppermint Filling. Combine 1½ cups cold milk and 2 teaspoons instant coffee granules in medium bowl; let stand 5 minutes. Add 1 package (4-serving size) instant vanilla pudding. Beat with electric mixer on lowest speed about 2 minutes or until well blended. Use as directed above to fill Chocolate Sponge Roll.

Chocolate Syrup Swirl Cake

MAKES 20 SERVINGS

- 1 cup (2 sticks) butter or margarine, softened
- 2 cups sugar
- 2 teaspoons vanilla extract
- 3 eggs
- 2¾ cups all-purpose flour
- 1¼ teaspoons baking soda, divided
- ½ teaspoon salt
- 1 cup buttermilk or sour milk*
- 1 cup HERSHEY'S Syrup
- 1 cup MOUNDS Sweetened Coconut Flakes (optional)

  To sour milk: Use 1 tablespoon white vinegar plus milk to equal 1 cup.

1. Heat oven to 350°F. Grease and flour 12-cup fluted tube pan or 10-inch tube pan.

2. Beat butter, sugar and vanilla with electric mixer in large bowl until fluffy. Add eggs; beat well. Stir together flour, 1 teaspoon baking soda and salt; add alternately with buttermilk to butter mixture, beating until well blended.

3. Measure 2 cups batter in small bowl; stir in syrup and remaining ¼ teaspoon baking soda. Add coconut, if desired, to remaining plain batter; pour into prepared pan. Pour chocolate batter over plain batter in pan; do not stir.

4. Bake 60 to 70 minutes or until wooden pick inserted in center comes out clean. Cool 15 minutes; remove from pan to wire rack. Cool completely; glaze or frost as desired.

Holiday Coconut Cake

MAKES 12 SERVINGS

COCONUT CAKE

½ cup (1 stick) butter or margarine, softened
½ cup shortening
2 cups sugar
5 eggs, separated
1 teaspoon vanilla extract
2 cups all-purpose flour
1 teaspoon baking soda
¼ teaspoon salt
1 cup buttermilk
2 cups MOUNDS Sweetened Coconut Flakes
½ cup chopped pecans

TOFFEE CREAM

2 cups cold whipping cream
¼ cup powdered sugar
1 teaspoon vanilla extract
½ cup HEATH BITS 'O BRICKLE Toffee Bits
Additional HEATH BITS 'O BRICKLE Toffee Bits (optional)

1. Heat oven to 350°F. Grease and flour 12-cup fluted tube pan.

2. Beat butter, shortening, sugar, egg yolks and vanilla until creamy. Add flour, baking soda and salt alternately with buttermilk, beating well. Stir in coconut and pecans.

3. Beat egg whites until stiff; fold into batter. Pour batter into prepared pan.

4. Bake 45 to 55 minutes or until wooden pick inserted in center comes out clean. Cool 10 minutes; remove from pan to wire rack. Cool completely.

5. For Toffee Cream, beat cold whipping cream, powdered sugar and vanilla extract with electric mixer on medium speed in large bowl until stiff. Fold in toffee bits. Garnish with additional toffee bits, if desired. Cover; store leftover cake in refrigerator.

HERSHEY'S SPECIAL DARK Truffle
Brownie Cheesecake

MAKES 10 TO 12 SERVINGS

BROWNIE LAYER

  6 tablespoons melted butter or margarine

$1\frac{1}{4}$ cups sugar

  1 teaspoon vanilla extract

  2 eggs

  1 cup plus 2 tablespoons all-purpose flour

$\frac{1}{3}$ cup HERSHEY'S Cocoa

$\frac{1}{2}$ teaspoon baking powder

$\frac{1}{2}$ teaspoon salt

TRUFFLE CHEESECAKE LAYER

  3 packages (8 oz. each) cream cheese, softened

$\frac{3}{4}$ cup sugar

  4 eggs

$\frac{1}{4}$ cup heavy cream

  2 teaspoons vanilla extract

$\frac{1}{4}$ teaspoon salt

  2 cups (12-oz. pkg.) HERSHEY'S SPECIAL DARK
     Chocolate Chips, divided

$\frac{1}{2}$ teaspoon shortening

1. Heat oven to 350°F. Grease 9-inch springform pan.

2. For Brownie Layer, stir together melted butter, sugar and vanilla extract. Add 2 eggs; stir until blended. Stir in all-purpose flour, cocoa, baking powder and ½ teaspoon salt; blend well. Spread in prepared pan. Bake 25 to 30 minutes or until brownie layer pulls away from sides of pan.

3. Meanwhile, for Truffle Cheesecake Layer, beat cream cheese and sugar with electric mixer on medium speed in large bowl until smooth. Gradually beat in eggs, heavy cream, vanilla and salt; continue beating until well blended.

4. Set aside 2 tablespoons chocolate chips. Place remaining chips in large microwave-safe bowl. Microwave at MEDIUM (50%) 1½ minutes or until smooth when stirred. Gradually blend melted chocolate into cheesecake batter.

5. Remove Brownie Layer from oven and immediately spoon cheesecake mixture over brownie. Return to oven; continue baking 45 to 50 minutes or until center is almost set. Remove from oven to wire rack. With knife, loosen cake from side of pan. Cool to room temperature. Remove side of pan.

6. Place remaining 2 tablespoons chocolate chips and shortening in small microwave-safe bowl. Microwave at MEDIUM (50%) 30 seconds or until chips are melted and smooth when stirred. Drizzle over top of cheesecake. Cover; refrigerate several hours until cold. Garnish as desired. Cover and refrigerate leftover cheesecake.

HERSHEY'S

Chocolate Cake Fingers
MAKES 42 PIECES

1 cup sugar*
1 cup all-purpose flour
⅓ cup HERSHEY'S Cocoa
¾ teaspoon baking powder
¾ teaspoon baking soda
½ cup nonfat milk
¼ cup frozen egg substitute, thawed
¼ cup canola oil or vegetable oil
1 teaspoon vanilla extract
½ cup boiling water
    Powdered sugar
1 teaspoon freshly grated orange peel
1½ cups frozen light nondairy whipped topping, thawed
42 fresh strawberries or raspberries (optional)

To reduce calories, replace up to half the sugar with an equivalent amount of sucralose sugar substitute. Reduce baking time about 3 minutes.

1. Heat oven to 350°F. Line bottom of 13×9×2-inch baking pan with waxed paper.

2. Stir together sugar, flour, cocoa, baking powder and baking soda in large bowl. Add milk, egg substitute, oil and vanilla; beat with electric mixer on medium speed for 2 minutes. Add water; stir with spoon until well blended. Pour batter into prepared pan.

3. Bake 16 to 18 minutes or until wooden pick inserted in center comes out clean. With knife or metal spatula, loosen cake from edges of pan. Place towel on wire rack; sprinkle lightly with powdered sugar. Invert cake on towel; peel off waxed paper. Cool completely. Invert cake, right side up, on cutting board. Cut cake into small rectangles (about 2×1¼ inches).

4. Stir orange peel into whipped topping; drop scant tablespoonful of topping on each piece of cake. Garnish with strawberry or raspberry, if desired. Store ungarnished cake, covered, at room temperature.

Cinnamon Chip
Applesauce Coffeecake

MAKES 12 TO 15 SERVINGS

1 cup (2 sticks) butter or margarine, softened
1 cup sugar
2 eggs
½ teaspoon vanilla extract
¾ cup applesauce
2½ cups all-purpose flour
1 teaspoon baking soda
½ teaspoon salt
1⅔ cups (10-oz. pkg.) HERSHEY'S Cinnamon Chips
1 cup chopped pecans (optional)
¾ cup powdered sugar
1 to 2 tablespoons warm water

1. Heat oven to 350°F. Lightly grease 13×9×2-inch baking pan.

2. Beat butter and sugar with electric mixer on medium speed in large bowl until well blended. Beat in eggs and vanilla. Mix in applesauce. Stir together flour, baking soda and salt; gradually add to butter mixture, beating until well blended. Stir in cinnamon chips and pecans, if desired. Spread in prepared pan.

3. Bake 30 to 35 minutes or until wooden pick inserted in center comes out clean. Cool in pan on wire rack. Stir together powdered sugar and warm water to make smooth glaze; drizzle cake with glaze or sprinkle with powdered sugar, as desired. Serve at room temperature or while still slightly warm.

VARIATIONS

FLUTED CAKE: Grease and flour 12-cup fluted tube pan. Prepare batter as directed; pour into prepared pan. Bake 45 to 50 minutes or until wooden pick inserted in thickest

part comes out clean. Cool 15 minutes; invert onto wire rack. Cool completely.

CUPCAKES: Line 24 baking cups (2½ inches in diameter) with paper baking liners. Prepare batter as directed; divide evenly into prepared cups. Bake 15 to 18 minutes or until wooden pick inserted in center comes out clean. Cool completely.

Chilled Raspberry Cheesecake

MAKES 10 TO 12 SERVINGS

CRUST

1½ cups (about 45 wafers) vanilla wafer crumbs
⅓ cup HERSHEY'S Cocoa
⅓ cup powdered sugar
⅓ cup butter or margarine, melted
3 tablespoons seedless red raspberry preserves

CHEESECAKE

1 package (10 oz.) frozen raspberries, thawed
1 envelope unflavored gelatin
½ cup cold water
½ cup boiling water
2 packages (8 oz. each) cream cheese, softened
½ cup granulated sugar
1 teaspoon vanilla extract

CHOCOLATE WHIPPED CREAM

½ cup powdered sugar
¼ cup HERSHEY'S Cocoa
1 cup whipping cream, cold
1 teaspoon vanilla extract
Fresh raspberries
Mint leaves (optional)

1. Heat oven to 350°F.

2. For Crust, stir together vanilla wafer crumbs, cocoa and powdered sugar in medium bowl; stir in melted butter. Press mixture onto bottom and 1½ inches up side of 9-inch springform pan. Bake 10 minutes; cool completely. Spread raspberry preserves over cooled crust.

3. For Cheesecake, purée and strain raspberries; set aside. Sprinkle gelatin over cold water in small bowl; let stand

several minutes to soften. Add boiling water; stir until gelatin dissolves completely and mixture is clear. Beat cream cheese, granulated sugar and vanilla with electric mixer in large bowl until smooth. Gradually add raspberry purée and gelatin mixture, mixing thoroughly; pour into prepared crust. Refrigerate several hours or overnight. Using knife, loosen cake from side of pan; remove side of pan.

4. For Chocolate Whipped Cream, combine powdered sugar and cocoa in medium bowl. Add whipping cream and vanilla extract; beat to stiff peaks with electric mixer. Garnish cheesecake with chocolate whipped cream, raspberries and mint, if desired. Cover; refrigerate leftover cheesecake.

Trimmed Down Chocoberry Cheesecake

MAKES 14 SERVINGS

GRAHAM CRUST

- ½ cup graham cracker crumbs
- 1 tablespoon melted margarine

CHOCOBERRY CHEESECAKE

- 1 container (8 oz.) nonfat cottage cheese
- 1 package (8 oz.) Neufchâtel cheese (⅓ less fat cream cheese)
- 1 cup sugar*
- ⅓ cup HERSHEY'S SPECIAL DARK Cocoa or HERSHEY'S Cocoa
- 1 package (10 oz.) frozen strawberries in syrup, thawed and thoroughly drained
- ⅓ cup liquid egg substitute
  Frozen light nondairy whipped topping, thawed (optional)
  Additional strawberries (optional)

To reduce calories, replace sugar with 1 cup sucralose sugar substitute.

1. For Graham Crust, stir together graham cracker crumbs and melted margarine; press into bottom of 8-inch springform pan.

2. For Chocoberry Cheesecake, heat oven to 325°F. Place cottage cheese in food processor; process until smooth. Add Neufchâtel cheese, sugar, cocoa and strawberries; process until smooth. Stir in egg substitute. Gently pour batter over prepared crust.

3. Bake 55 to 60 minutes or just until almost set in center. With knife, loosen cheesecake from side of pan. Cool completely in pan on wire rack. Cover; refrigerate until chilled. Just before serving, remove side of pan. Serve with whipped topping and additional strawberries, if desired. Cover; refrigerate leftover cheesecake.

SIMPLY SATISFYING SWEETS

HERSHEY'S

Brownies
& BARS

Chocolate-Almond Honeys

MAKES 20 BARS

1¾ cups graham cracker crumbs
1 can (14 oz.) sweetened condensed milk
   (not evaporated milk)
2 tablespoons honey
2 tablespoons orange or apple juice
1 teaspoon freshly grated orange peel
1 cup HERSHEY'S SPECIAL DARK Chocolate Chips or
   HERSHEY'S Semi-Sweet Chocolate Chips
½ cup chopped blanched almonds

1. Heat oven to 350°F. Grease 9-inch square baking pan.

2. Stir together graham cracker crumbs, sweetened condensed milk, honey, orange juice and orange peel in large bowl. Stir in chocolate chips and almonds. Spread batter in prepared pan.

3. Bake 30 minutes or until golden brown. Cool completely in pan on wire rack. Cut into bars.

Chewy Toffee Almond Bars

MAKES 36 BARS

- 1 cup (2 sticks) butter, softened
- ½ cup sugar
- 2 cups all-purpose flour
- 1⅓ cups (8-oz. pkg.) HEATH BITS 'O BRICKLE Toffee Bits
- ¾ cup light corn syrup
- 1 cup sliced almonds, divided
- ¾ cup MOUNDS Sweetened Coconut Flakes, divided

1. Heat oven to 350°F. Grease sides of 13×9×2-inch baking pan.

2. Beat butter and sugar with electric mixer until fluffy. Gradually add flour, beating until well blended. Press dough evenly into prepared pan. Bake 15 to 20 minutes or until edges are lightly browned.

3. Meanwhile, combine toffee bits and corn syrup in medium saucepan. Cook over medium heat, stirring constantly, until toffee is melted (about 10 to 12 minutes). Stir in ½ cup almonds and ½ cup coconut. Spread toffee mixture to within ¼ inch of edges of crust. Sprinkle remaining ½ cup almonds and remaining ¼ cup coconut over top.

4. Bake an additional 15 minutes or until bubbly. Cool completely in pan on wire rack. Cut into bars.

Chocolate Orange Cheesecake Bars

MAKES 24 BARS

CRUST

- 1 cup all-purpose flour
- ½ cup packed light brown sugar
- ¼ teaspoon ground cinnamon (optional)
- ⅓ cup shortening
- ½ cup chopped pecans

CHOCOLATE ORANGE FILLING

- 1 package (8 oz.) cream cheese, softened
- ⅔ cup sugar
- ⅓ cup HERSHEY'S Cocoa
- ¼ cup milk
- 1 egg
- 1 teaspoon vanilla extract
- ¼ teaspoon freshly grated orange peel
- Pecan halves (optional)

1. Heat oven to 350°F.

2. For Crust, stir together flour, brown sugar and cinnamon in large bowl. Cut shortening into flour mixture with pastry blender or two knives until mixture resembles coarse crumbs. Stir in chopped pecans. Reserve ¾ cup flour mixture. Press remaining mixture firmly onto bottom of ungreased 9-inch square baking pan. Bake 10 minutes or until lightly browned.

3. For Chocolate Orange Filling, beat cream cheese and sugar in medium bowl with electric mixer until fluffy. Add cocoa, milk, egg, vanilla and orange peel; beat until smooth.

4. Spread filling over warm crust. Sprinkle with reserved flour mixture. Press pecan halves lightly onto top, if desired. Return to oven. Bake 25 to 30 minutes or until lightly browned. Cool; cut into bars. Cover; refrigerate leftover bars.

White Chip Lemon Streusel Bars

MAKES 36 BARS

1 can (14 oz.) sweetened condensed milk (not evaporated milk)
½ cup lemon juice
1 teaspoon freshly grated lemon peel
2 cups (12-oz pkg.) HERSHEY'S Premier White Chips, divided
⅔ cup butter or margarine, softened
1 cup packed light brown sugar
1½ cups all-purpose flour
1½ cups regular rolled or quick-cooking oats
¾ cup toasted pecan pieces*
1 teaspoon baking powder
½ teaspoon salt
1 egg
½ teaspoon shortening

To toast pecans: Heat oven to 350°F. Spread pecans in thin layer in shallow baking pan. Bake, stirring occasionally, 7 to 8 minutes or until golden brown; cool.

1. Heat oven to 350°F. Lightly grease 13×9×2-inch baking pan. Combine sweetened condensed milk, lemon juice and lemon peel in medium bowl; set aside. Measure out ¼ cup and ⅓ cup white chips; set aside. Add remaining white chips to lemon mixture.

2. Beat butter and brown sugar until blended in large mixer bowl. Stir together flour, oats, pecans, baking powder and salt; add to butter mixture, blending well. Remove 1⅔ cups oats mixture; set aside. Add egg to remaining mixture, blending until crumbly. Press egg/crumb mixture on bottom of prepared pan. Gently spoon lemon mixture on top, spreading evenly. Add reserved ⅓ cup white chips to reserved crumb mixture. Sprinkle over lemon layer, pressing crumbs down lightly.

3. Bake 20 to 25 minutes or until lightly browned. Cool in pan on wire rack. Place remaining ¼ cup white chips and shortening in small microwave-safe bowl. Microwave at MEDIUM (50%) 30 seconds or until chips are melted and mixture is smooth when stirred. Drizzle over baked bars. Allow drizzle to set; cut into bars.

Peanut Butter Fudge Brownie Bars

MAKES 36 BARS

- 1 cup (2 sticks) butter or margarine, melted
- 1½ cups sugar
- 2 eggs
- 1 teaspoon vanilla extract
- 1¼ cups all-purpose flour
- ⅔ cup HERSHEY'S Cocoa
- ¼ cup milk
- 1¼ cups chopped pecans or walnuts, divided
- ½ cup (1 stick) butter or margarine
- 1⅔ cups (10-oz. pkg.) REESE'S Peanut Butter Chips
- 1 can (14 oz.) sweetened condensed milk (not evaporated milk)
- ¼ cup HERSHEY'S SPECIAL DARK Chocolate Chips or HERSHEY'S Semi-Sweet Chocolate Chips

1. Heat oven to 350°F. Grease 13×9×2-inch baking pan.

2. Combine melted butter, sugar, eggs and vanilla in large bowl; beat well. Add flour, cocoa and milk; beat until blended. Stir in 1 cup nuts. Spread in prepared pan.

3. Bake 25 to 30 minutes or just until edges begin to pull away from sides of pan. Cool completely in pan on wire rack.

4. Melt ½ cup butter and peanut butter chips in medium saucepan over low heat, stirring constantly. Add sweetened condensed milk, stirring until smooth; pour over baked layer.

5. Place chocolate chips in small microwave-safe bowl. Microwave at MEDIUM (50%) 45 seconds or just until chips are melted when stirred. Drizzle bars with melted chocolate; sprinkle with remaining ¼ cup nuts. Refrigerate 1 hour or until firm. Cut into bars. Cover; refrigerate leftover bars.

Rich Chocolate Chip Toffee Bars

MAKES 48 BARS

2⅓ cups all-purpose flour
⅔ cup packed light brown sugar
¾ cup (1½ sticks) butter or margarine
1 egg, lightly beaten
2 cups (12-oz. pkg.) HERSHEY'S SPECIAL DARK Chocolate Chips or HERSHEY'S Semi-Sweet Chocolate Chips, divided
1 cup coarsely chopped nuts
1 can (14 oz.) sweetened condensed milk (not evaporated milk)
1⅓ cups (8-oz. pkg.) HEATH BITS 'O BRICKLE Toffee Bits, divided

1. Heat oven to 350°F. Grease 13×9×2-inch baking pan.

2. Combine flour and brown sugar in large bowl. Cut butter into flour mixture with pastry blender or two knives until mixture resembles coarse crumbs. Add egg; mix well. Stir in 1½ cups chocolate chips and nuts; set aside 1½ cups mixture.

3. Press remaining crumb mixture onto bottom of prepared pan. Bake 10 minutes. Pour sweetened condensed milk evenly over hot crust; set aside ¼ cup toffee bits. Sprinkle remaining toffee bits over sweetened condensed milk. Sprinkle reserved crumb mixture and remaining ½ cup chips over top.

4. Bake 25 to 30 minutes or until golden brown. Top with reserved toffee bits. Cool completely in pan on wire rack. Cut into bars.

Mini KISSES Fruit Bars

MAKES 36 BARS

1½ cups all-purpose flour
1½ cups quick-cooking rolled oats
  1 cup packed light brown sugar
  1 teaspoon baking powder
  ¾ cup (1½ sticks) butter or margarine, softened
  1 jar (10 to 12 oz.) raspberry jam
1¾ cups (10-oz. pkg.) HERSHEY'S Mini KISSES BRAND
     Milk Chocolates
  ½ cup chopped nuts (optional)

1. Heat oven to 350°F. Lightly grease 13×9×2-inch baking pan.

2. Combine flour, oats, brown sugar and baking powder in large bowl. Cut butter into flour mixture with pastry blender or two knives until mixture resembles coarse crumbs. Remove 2 cups crumb mixture; set aside.

3. Press remaining crumb mixture onto bottom of prepared pan. Stir jam to soften; carefully spread over crumb mixture. Sprinkle chocolates evenly over jam. Cover with reserved crumbs. Sprinkle nuts over top, if desired; press down firmly.

4. Bake 40 to 45 minutes or until lightly browned. Cool completely in pan on wire rack. Cut into bars.

Mini Brownie Cups

MAKES 24 BROWNIES

BROWNIE CUPS

- ¼ cup (½ stick) reduced-fat margarine, melted and cooled
- 2 egg whites
- 1 egg
- ¾ cup sugar*
- ⅔ cup all-purpose flour
- ⅓ cup HERSHEY'S Cocoa
- ½ teaspoon baking powder
- ¼ teaspoon salt

MOCHA GLAZE

- ¼ cup powdered sugar
- ¾ teaspoon HERSHEY'S Cocoa
- ¼ teaspoon powdered instant coffee
- 2 teaspoons hot water
- ¼ teaspoon vanilla extract

To reduce calories, replace up to half the sugar with an equivalent amount of sucralose sugar substitute (sold as Splenda®). Reduce baking time by 2 to 3 minutes.

1. For Brownie Cups, heat oven to 350°F. Line small muffin cups (1¾ inches in diameter) with paper baking cups or spray with vegetable cooking spray.

2. Beat egg whites and egg with electric mixer on medium speed in small bowl until foamy; gradually add sugar, beating until slightly thickened and light in color.

3. Stir together flour, cocoa, baking powder and salt; add gradually to egg mixture with mixer running, beating until blended. Gradually beat in melted margarine, mixing just until blended. Fill muffin cups ⅔ full with batter. Bake 15 to 18 minutes or until wooden pick inserted in center comes out clean. Remove from pan to wire rack. Cool completely.

4. For Mocha Glaze, stir together powdered sugar and cocoa in small bowl. Dissolve coffee in water; add to sugar mixture, stirring until well blended. Stir in vanilla.

5. Drizzle Brownie Cups with glaze; let stand until glaze sets. Store, covered, at room temperature.

Toffee-Topped Cheesecake Bars

MAKES 36 BARS

1⅓ cups all-purpose flour
1 cup powdered sugar
⅓ cup HERSHEY'S Cocoa
¼ teaspoon baking soda
¾ cup (1½ sticks) butter or margarine, softened
1 package (8 oz.) cream cheese, softened
1 can (14 oz.) sweetened condensed milk (not
   evaporated milk)
2 eggs
1 teaspoon vanilla extract
1⅓ cups (8-oz. pkg.) HEATH BITS 'O BRICKLE Toffee Bits,
   divided

1. Heat oven to 350°F.

2. Combine flour, powdered sugar, cocoa and baking soda in medium bowl; cut butter into flour mixture with pastry blender or two knives until mixture resembles coarse crumbs. Press into bottom of ungreased 13×9×2-inch baking pan. Bake 15 minutes.

3. Beat cream cheese until fluffy. Add sweetened condensed milk, eggs and vanilla; beat until smooth. Stir in ¾ cup toffee bits. Pour mixture over hot crust. Bake 20 to 25 minutes or until set and edges just begin to brown.

4. Remove from oven. Cool 15 minutes. Sprinkle remaining toffee bits evenly over top. Cool completely. Refrigerate several hours or until cold. Cover; store leftover bars in refrigerator.

Fudgey SPECIAL DARK Brownies

MAKES 36 BROWNIES

¾ cup HERSHEY'S Cocoa
½ teaspoon baking soda
⅔ cup butter or margarine, melted and divided
½ cup boiling water
2 cups sugar
2 eggs
1⅓ cups all-purpose flour
1 teaspoon vanilla extract
¼ teaspoon salt
1 cup HERSHEY'S SPECIAL DARK Chocolate Chips

1. Heat oven to 350°F. Grease 13×9×2-inch baking pan.

2. Stir together cocoa and baking soda in large bowl; stir in ⅓ cup butter. Add boiling water; stir until mixture thickens. Stir in sugar, eggs and remaining ⅓ cup butter; stir until smooth. Add flour, vanilla and salt; blend completely. Stir in chocolate chips. Pour into prepared pan.

3. Bake 35 to 40 minutes or until brownies begin to pull away from sides of pan. Cool completely in pan on wire rack. Frost, if desired. Cut into squares.

SPECIAL DARK Fudge Fondue

MAKES 1 ½ CUPS FONDUE

- 2 cups (12-oz pkg.) HERSHEY'S SPECIAL DARK Chocolate Chips
- ½ cup light cream
- 2 teaspoons vanilla extract
  Assorted fondue dippers such as marshmallows, cherries, grapes, mandarin orange segments, pineapple chunks, strawberries, slices of other fresh fruits, small pieces of cake or small brownies

1. Place chocolate chips and light cream in medium microwave-safe bowl. Microwave at MEDIUM (50%) 1 minute or just until chips are melted and mixture is smooth when stirred. Stir in vanilla.

2. Pour into fondue pot or chafing dish; serve warm with fondue dippers. If mixture thickens, stir in additional light cream, one tablespoon at a time. Refrigerate leftover fondue.

STOVETOP DIRECTIONS: Combine chocolate chips and light cream in heavy medium saucepan. Cook over low heat, stirring constantly, until chips are melted and mixture is hot. Stir in vanilla, and continue as in Step 2 above.

SPECIAL CELEBRATION TREATS

Chocolate Coconut Balls

MAKES ABOUT 4 DOZEN CANDIES

6 sections (½ oz. each) HERSHEY'S Unsweetened Chocolate Premium Baking Bar
¼ cup (½ stick) butter
½ cup sweetened condensed milk (not evaporated milk)
¾ cup granulated sugar
¼ cup water
1 tablespoon light corn syrup
1 teaspoon vanilla extract
2 cups MOUNDS Sweetened Coconut Flakes
1 cup chopped nuts
   Powdered sugar

1. Melt chocolate and butter in large heavy saucepan over very low heat. Add sweetened condensed milk; stir to blend. Remove from heat.

2. Combine granulated sugar, water and corn syrup in small saucepan. Cook over medium heat, stirring constantly, until sugar is dissolved. Cook, without stirring, until mixture reaches 250°F on candy thermometer or until a small amount of syrup dropped into very cold water forms a firm ball which does not flatten when removed from water. (Do not allow bulb of candy thermometer to rest on bottom of saucepan.) Remove from heat; stir into chocolate mixture. Add vanilla, coconut and nuts; stir until well blended.

3. Refrigerate about 1 hour or until firm enough to handle. Shape into 1-inch balls; roll in powdered sugar. Store tightly covered in cool, dry place.

NOTE: For best results, do not double this recipe.

Chips and Bits Cookie Pie

MAKES 8 SERVINGS

½ cup (1 stick) butter or margarine, softened
2 eggs, beaten
2 teaspoons vanilla extract
1 cup sugar
½ cup all-purpose flour
1 cup HERSHEY'S SPECIAL DARK Chocolate Chips or
   HERSHEY'S Semi-Sweet Chocolate Chips
½ cup HEATH BITS 'O BRICKLE Toffee Bits
½ cup chopped pecans or walnuts
1 unbaked (9-inch) pie crust
   Ice cream or whipped cream (optional)

1. Heat oven to 350°F.

2. Beat butter with electric mixer on medium speed in large bowl until fluffy. Add eggs and vanilla; beat thoroughly. Stir together sugar and flour; add to butter mixture, mixing until well blended. Stir in chocolate chips, toffee bits and nuts; spread in unbaked pie crust.

3. Bake 45 to 50 minutes or until golden. Cool about one hour before serving; serve warm, or reheat cooled pie slices by microwaving at HIGH (100%) for about 10 seconds. Serve with ice cream or whipped cream, if desired.

Chocolate Pecan Pie

MAKES 8 SERVINGS

1 cup sugar
⅓ cup HERSHEY'S Cocoa
3 eggs, lightly beaten
¾ cup light corn syrup
1 tablespoon butter or margarine, melted
1 teaspoon vanilla extract
1 cup pecan halves
1 unbaked (9-inch) pie crust
Whipped topping

1. Heat oven to 350°F.

2. Stir together sugar and cocoa in medium bowl. Add eggs, corn syrup, butter and vanilla; stir until well blended. Stir in pecans. Pour into unbaked pie crust.

3. Bake 60 minutes or until set. Remove from oven to wire rack. Cool completely. Garnish with whipped topping.

Classic Chocolate Cream Pie

MAKES 8 TO 10 SERVINGS

5 sections (½ oz. each) HERSHEY'S Unsweetened
   Chocolate Premium Baking Bar, broken into pieces
3 cups milk, divided
1⅓ cups sugar
3 tablespoons all-purpose flour
3 tablespoons cornstarch
½ teaspoon salt
3 egg yolks
2 tablespoons butter or margarine
1½ teaspoons vanilla extract
1 baked (9-inch) pie crust, cooled, or 1 (9-inch)
   crumb crust
Sweetened whipped cream (optional)

1. Combine chocolate and 2 cups milk in medium saucepan; cook over medium heat, stirring constantly, just until mixture boils. Remove from heat and set aside.

2. Stir together sugar, flour, cornstarch and salt in medium bowl, whisk remaining 1 cup milk into egg yolks in separate bowl; stir into sugar mixture. Gradually add to chocolate mixture. Cook over medium heat, whisking constantly, until mixture boils; boil and stir 1 minute. Remove from heat; stir in butter and vanilla.

3. Pour into prepared pastry shell; press plastic wrap directly onto surface. Cool; refrigerate until well chilled. Top with whipped cream, if desired.

Lighter Than Air Chocolate Delight

MAKES 8 SERVINGS

 2 envelopes unflavored gelatin
½ cup cold water
 1 cup boiling water
1⅓ cups nonfat dry milk powder
⅓ cup HERSHEY'S SPECIAL DARK Cocoa or
      HERSHEY'S Cocoa
 1 tablespoon vanilla extract
    Dash salt
    Granulated sugar substitute to equal 14 teaspoons
      sugar
 8 large ice cubes

1. Sprinkle gelatin over cold water in blender container; let stand 4 minutes to soften. Gently stir with rubber spatula, scraping gelatin particles off sides; add boiling water to gelatin mixture. Cover; blend until gelatin dissolves. Add dry milk powder, cocoa, vanilla and salt; blend on medium speed until well mixed. Add sugar substitute and ice cubes; blend on high speed until ice is crushed and mixture is smooth and fluffy.

2. Immediately pour into 4-cup mold. Cover; refrigerate until firm. Unmold onto serving plate just before serving.

NOTE: Eight individual dessert dishes may be used in place of 4-cup mold, if desired.

HERSHEY'S Premier White Chips Almond Fudge

MAKES ABOUT 3 DOZEN PIECES
OR 1 ½ POUNDS FUDGE

2 cups (12-oz. pkg.) HERSHEY'S Premier White Chips

⅔ cup sweetened condensed milk (not evaporated milk)

1½ cups coarsely chopped slivered almonds, toasted*

½ teaspoon vanilla extract

*To toast almonds: Spread almonds on cookie sheet. Bake at 350°F, stirring occasionally, 8 to 10 minutes or until lightly browned; remove from cookie sheet immediately and cool completely.

1. Line 8-inch square pan with foil, extending foil over edges of pan.

2. Melt white chips with sweetened condensed milk in medium saucepan over very low heat, stirring constantly, until mixture is smooth.

3. Remove from heat. Stir in almonds and vanilla. Spread in prepared pan. Cover; refrigerate 2 hours or until firm. Use foil to lift fudge out of pan; peel off foil. Cut fudge into 1¼-inch squares.

NOTE: For best results, do not double this recipe.

SPECIAL DARK Fudge Truffles

MAKES ABOUT 3 DOZEN TRUFFLES

2 cups (12-oz. pkg.) HERSHEY'S SPECIAL DARK
   Chocolate Chips
¾ cup whipping cream
   Various coatings such as toasted chopped pecans,
   coconut, powdered sugar, cocoa or small candy
   pieces

1. Combine chocolate chips and whipping cream in
medium microwave-safe bowl. Microwave at MEDIUM
(50%) 1 minute; stir. If necessary, microwave at MEDIUM
an additional 15 seconds at a time, stirring after each heating,
until chips are melted and mixture is smooth when stirred.

2. Refrigerate 3 hours or until firm. Roll mixture into 1-inch
balls. Roll each ball in coatings as desired. Cover; refrigerate
until serving.

Deep Dark Mousse

MAKES 4 TO 6 SERVINGS

¼ cup sugar
1 teaspoon unflavored gelatin
½ cup milk
1 cup HERSHEY'S SPECIAL DARK Chocolate Chips
2 teaspoons vanilla extract
1 cup cold whipping cream
   Sweetened whipped cream (optional)

1. Stir together sugar and gelatin in small saucepan; stir
in milk. Let stand 2 minutes to soften gelatin. Cook over
medium heat, stirring constantly, until mixture just begins
to boil.

2. Remove from heat. Immediately add chocolate chips;

stir until melted. Stir in vanilla; cool to room temperature.

3. Beat whipping cream with electric mixer on medium speed in large bowl until stiff. Add half chocolate mixture and gently fold until nearly combined; add remaining chocolate mixture and fold just until blended. Spoon into serving dish or individual dishes. Refrigerate. Garnish with sweetened whipped cream, if desired, just before serving.

Toffee Popcorn Crunch
MAKES ABOUT 1 POUND POPCORN

- 8 **cups popped popcorn**
- ¾ **cup whole or slivered almonds**
- 1⅓ **cups (8-oz pkg.) HEATH BITS 'O BRICKLE Toffee Bits**
- ½ **cup light corn syrup**

1. Heat oven to 275°F. Grease large roasting pan (or two 13×9×2-inch baking pans). Place popcorn and almonds in prepared pan.

2. Combine toffee bits and corn syrup in heavy medium saucepan. Cook over medium heat, stirring constantly, until toffee melts (about 12 minutes). Pour over popcorn mixture; stir until evenly coated.

3. Bake 30 minutes, stirring frequently. Remove from oven; stir every 2 minutes until slightly cooled. Cool completely. Store in tightly covered container in cool, dry place.

NOTE: For best results, do not double this recipe.

Milk Chocolate Pots de Crème

MAKES ABOUT 6 TO 8 SERVINGS

2 cups (11½-oz. pkg.) HERSHEY'S Milk Chocolate
  Chips
½ cup light cream
½ teaspoon vanilla extract
  Sweetened whipped cream

1. Place milk chocolate chips and light cream in medium microwave-safe bowl. Microwave at MEDIUM (50%) 1 minute; stir. If necessary, microwave at MEDIUM an additional 15 seconds at a time, stirring after each heating, just until chocolate is melted and smooth when stirred. Stir in vanilla.

2. Pour into demitasse cups or very small dessert dishes. Cover; refrigerate until firm. Serve cold with sweetened whipped cream.

Butterscotch Nut Fudge

MAKES ABOUT 5 DOZEN PIECES
OR ABOUT 2¼ POUNDS CANDY

1¾ cups sugar
1 jar (7 oz.) marshmallow crème
¾ cup evaporated milk
¼ cup (½ stick) butter
1¾ cups (11-oz. pkg.) HERSHEY'S Butterscotch Chips
1 cup chopped salted mixed nuts
1 teaspoon vanilla extract

1. Line 8-inch square pan with foil, extending foil over edges of pan.

2. Combine sugar, marshmallow crème, evaporated milk and butter in heavy 3-quart saucepan. Cook over medium heat, stirring constantly, until mixture comes to full boil; boil and stir 5 minutes.

3. Remove from heat; gradually add butterscotch chips, stirring until chips are melted. Stir in nuts and vanilla. Pour into prepared pan; cool.

4. Refrigerate 2 to 3 hours. Remove from pan; place on cutting board. Peel off foil. Cut into squares. Store tightly covered in refrigerator.

Hot Merry Mocha

MAKES ABOUT 10 (6-OUNCE) SERVINGS

6 tablespoons HERSHEY'S Cocoa
1 to 2 tablespoons powdered instant coffee
⅛ teaspoon salt
6 cups hot water
1 can (14 oz.) sweetened condensed milk
   (not evaporated milk)
Sweetened whipped cream (optional)

1. Combine cocoa, instant coffee and salt in 4-quart saucepan; stir in water.

2. Cook over medium heat, stirring occasionally, until mixture boils. Stir in sweetened condensed milk. Heat thoroughly; do not boil. Beat with whisk until foamy. Serve hot, topped with whipped cream, if desired.

VARIATION: Minted Hot Chocolate: Follow directions above, omitting instant coffee. Stir in ¼ to ½ teaspoon mint extract before beating. Serve with candy cane for stirrer, if desired.

Premium Chocolate Mint Sauce

MAKES ABOUT 2 CUPS SAUCE

1⅔ cups (10-oz. pkg.) HERSHEY'S Mint Chocolate Chips
1 cup whipping cream
½ teaspoon vanilla extract
Ice cream, cake or other desserts

Combine mint chocolate chips and whipping cream in small saucepan. Cook over very low heat, stirring constantly, until chocolate is melted and mixture is smooth; remove from heat. Stir in vanilla. Serve warm sauce over ice cream or desserts.

MICROWAVE DIRECTIONS: Place mint chocolate chips and whipping cream in medium microwave-safe bowl. Microwave at MEDIUM (50%) 1 minute; stir. If necessary, microwave at MEDIUM an additional 15 seconds at a time, stirring after each heating, until chips are melted and mixture is smooth when stirred. Stir in vanilla; serve as directed.

HERSHEY'S®

DECADENT DELIGHTS

HERSHEY'S

Contents

HERSHEY'S

Brownies
& Bars

Thick and Fudgey Brownies with HERSHEY'S Mini KISSES Milk Chocolates

Makes 24 brownies

- 2¼ **cups all-purpose flour**
- ⅔ **cup HERSHEY'S Cocoa**
- 1 **teaspoon baking powder**
- 1 **teaspoon salt**
- ¾ **cup (1½ sticks) butter or margarine, melted**
- 2½ **cups sugar**
- 2 **teaspoons vanilla extract**
- 4 **eggs**
- 1¾ **cups (10-oz. pkg.) HERSHEY'S Mini KISSES**BRAND **Milk Chocolates**

1. Heat oven to 350°F. (325°F for glass baking dish). Grease 13×9×2-inch baking pan.

2. Stir together flour, cocoa, baking powder and salt. With spoon or whisk, stir together butter, sugar and vanilla in large bowl. Add eggs; stir until well blended. Stir in flour mixture, blending well. Stir in chocolate pieces. Spread batter in prepared pan.

3. Bake 30 to 35 minutes or until brownies begin to pull away from sides of pan. Cool completely in pan on wire rack; cut into 2-inch squares.

HERSHEY'S

Championship Chocolate Chip Bars

Makes 36 bars

- 1½ cups all-purpose flour
- ½ cup packed light brown sugar
- ½ cup (1 stick) cold butter or margarine
- 2 cups (12-oz. pkg.) HERSHEY'S SPECIAL DARK Chocolate Chips or HERSHEY'S Semi-Sweet Chocolate Chips, divided
- 1 can (14 oz.) sweetened condensed milk (not evaporated milk)
- 1 egg, slightly beaten
- 1 teaspoon vanilla extract
- 1 cup chopped nuts

1. Heat oven to 350°F.

2. Stir together flour and brown sugar in medium bowl; cut in cold butter until crumbly. Stir in ½ cup chocolate chips; press mixture on bottom of ungreased 13×9×2-inch baking pan. Bake 15 minutes.

3. Combine sweetened condensed milk, egg and vanilla in large bowl. Stir in remaining 1½ cups chips and nuts. Spread evenly over hot baked crust. Bake 25 minutes or until golden. Cool in pan on wire rack then cut into bars.

HERSHEY'S

Rocky Road Brownies

Makes about 20 brownies

  1 cup HERSHEY'S SPECIAL DARK Chocolate Chips or
     HERSHEY'S Semi-Sweet Chocolate Chips
1¼ cups miniature marshmallows
  ½ cup chopped nuts
  ½ cup (1 stick) butter or margarine
  1 cup sugar
  1 teaspoon vanilla extract
  2 eggs
  ½ cup all-purpose flour
  ⅓ cup HERSHEY'S Cocoa
  ½ teaspoon baking powder
  ½ teaspoon salt

1. Heat oven to 350°F. Grease 9-inch square baking pan.

2. Stir together chocolate chips, marshmallows and nuts; set aside. Place butter in large microwave-safe bowl. Microwave at HIGH (100%) 1 to 1½ minutes or until melted. Add sugar, vanilla and eggs; beat with spoon until well blended. Add flour, cocoa, baking powder and salt; stir until well blended. Spread batter in prepared pan.

3. Bake 22 minutes. Sprinkle chocolate chip mixture over top. Continue baking 5 minutes or until marshmallows have softened and puffed slightly. Cool completely in pan on wire rack. Using wet knife, cut into squares.

HERSHEY'S

Chippy Chewy Bars

Makes 48 bars

½ cup (1 stick) butter or margarine

1½ cups graham cracker crumbs

1⅔ cups (10-oz. pkg.) REESE'S Peanut Butter Chips, divided

1½ cups MOUNDS Sweetened Coconut Flakes

1 can (14 oz.) sweetened condensed milk (not evaporated milk)

1 cup HERSHEY'S SPECIAL DARK Chocolate Chips, HERSHEY'S Semi-Sweet Chocolate Chips or HERSHEY'S Mini Chips Semi-Sweet Chocolate

1½ teaspoons shortening (do not use butter, margarine, spread or oil)

1. Heat oven to 350°F. Place butter in 13×9×2-inch baking pan. Heat in oven until melted; remove pan from oven. Sprinkle graham cracker crumbs evenly over butter; press down with fork.

2. Sprinkle 1 cup peanut butter chips over crumbs; sprinkle coconut over chips. Layer remaining ⅔ cup peanut butter chips over coconut; drizzle sweetened condensed milk evenly over top. Press down firmly.

3. Bake 20 minutes or until lightly browned.

4. Combine chocolate chips and shortening in small microwave-safe bowl. Microwave at MEDIUM (50%) 1 minute; stir. If necessary, microwave at MEDIUM an additional 15 seconds at a time, stirring after each heating, just until chips are melted and mixture is smooth. Drizzle evenly over top of baked mixture. Cool completely. Cut into bars.

NOTE: For a lighter drizzle, use ½ cup chocolate chips and ¾ teaspoon shortening. Microwave at MEDIUM 30 seconds to 1 minute or until chips are melted when stirred.

HERSHEY'S

Peanut Butter Chip Fruit Bars

Makes 24 bars

1½	cups REESE'S Peanut Butter Chips, divided
1	package (8 oz.) cream cheese, softened
1	cup packed light brown sugar
1	egg
1	teaspoon vanilla extract
1	cup all-purpose flour
½	teaspoon baking soda
¼	teaspoon salt
½	cup quick-cooking oats
1	cup chopped dried mixed fruit, or dried fruit bits
1	cup powdered sugar
2	tablespoons orange juice
¼	teaspoon freshly grated orange peel (optional)

1. Heat oven to 350°F. Grease 13×9×2-inch baking pan.

2. Place 1 cup peanut butter chips in microwave-safe bowl. Microwave at MEDIUM (50%) 1 minute; stir. If necessary, microwave an additional 15 seconds at a time, stirring after each heating, until chips are melted and smooth when stirred. Beat melted peanut butter chips and cream cheese in large bowl until well blended. Add brown sugar, egg and vanilla; blend well. Stir together flour, baking soda and salt; add to cream cheese mixture, blending well. Stir in oats, remaining ½ cup peanut butter chips and dried fruit.

3. Spread batter in prepared pan. Bake 20 to 25 minutes or until golden brown. Cool in pan on wire rack.

4. Meanwhile, stir together powdered sugar, orange juice and grated orange peel in small mixing bowl; blend until smooth. (Add additional orange juice, a teaspoonful at a time, if glaze is too thick.) Pour over bars and cool completely. Cut into bars.

HERSHEY'S

English Toffee Bars

Makes 36 bars

2 cups all-purpose flour
1⅓ cups packed light brown sugar, divided
½ plus ⅔ cup cold butter, divided
1 cup pecan halves
1 cup HERSHEY'S Milk Chocolate Chips

1. Heat oven to 350°F.

2. Combine flour and 1 cup brown sugar in large bowl. With pastry blender or fork, cut in ½ cup butter until fine crumbs form (a few large crumbs may remain). Press mixture onto bottom of ungreased 13×9×2-inch baking pan. Sprinkle pecans over crust. Set aside.

3. Combine remaining ⅓ cup brown sugar and ⅔ cup butter in small saucepan over medium heat. Cook, stirring constantly, until mixture comes to a boil. Boil 30 seconds, stirring constantly, then immediately pour over pecans and crust.

4. Bake 20 to 22 minutes or until topping is bubbly and golden; remove from oven. Immediately sprinkle milk chocolate chips evenly over top; press gently onto surface. Cool completely in pan on wire rack. Cut into bars.

HERSHEY'S

Chocolate and Pecan Bars

Makes 24 bars

- 1 cup all-purpose flour
- 1 cup graham cracker crumbs
- ⅔ cup sugar
- ½ teaspoon salt
- ¾ cup (1½ sticks) butter or margarine
- 2 eggs, divided
- 1 can (14 oz.) sweetened condensed milk (not evaporated milk)
- ½ cup HERSHEY'S Cocoa
- 1½ teaspoons vanilla extract
- ½ cup MOUNDS Sweetened Coconut Flakes
- 1 cup chopped pecans

1. Heat oven to 350°F.

2. Stir together flour, graham cracker crumbs, sugar and salt in large bowl. Add butter; cut in until mixture resembles coarse crumbs.

3. Beat 1 egg in small bowl. Stir into flour mixture. Press mixture evenly onto bottom of ungreased 13×9×2-inch baking pan. Bake 25 minutes or until golden.

4. Meanwhile, beat sweetened condensed milk, cocoa, remaining egg and vanilla in medium bowl. Pour over baked layer and sprinkle with coconut, then pecans.

5. Bake 25 minutes or until set. Cool completely in pan on wire rack. Cut into bars.

HERSHEY'S

Chewy Black Forest Bars

Makes 48 bars

1 cup (2 sticks) butter or margarine

¾ cup HERSHEY'S Cocoa or HERSHEY'S SPECIAL DARK Cocoa

2 cups sugar

4 eggs, divided

1½ cups plus ⅓ cup all-purpose flour, divided

⅓ cup chopped almonds

1 can (14 oz.) sweetened condensed milk (not evaporated milk)

½ teaspoon almond extract

1 cup HERSHEY'S SPECIAL DARK Chocolate Chips, HERSHEY'S Semi-Sweet Chocolate Chips or HERSHEY'S Milk Chocolate Chips

¾ cup chopped candied red cherries

1. Heat oven to 350°F. Generously grease 13×9×2-inch baking pan.

2. Melt butter in large saucepan over low heat; stir in cocoa until smooth. Remove from heat. Add sugar, 3 eggs, 1½ cups flour and almonds; mix well. Pour into prepared pan. Bake 15 minutes.

3. Meanwhile, whisk together remaining 1 egg, ⅓ cup flour, sweetened condensed milk and almond extract. Pour over baked layer; sprinkle chocolate chips and cherries over top. Return to oven. Bake 25 to 30 minutes or until set and edges are golden brown. Cool completely in pan on wire rack. Refrigerate until cold, 6 hours or overnight. Cut into bars. Cover and refrigerate leftover bars.

HERSHEY'S

Marbled Cheesecake Bars

Makes 24 to 36 bars

2 cups vanilla wafer crumbs (about 60 wafers, crushed)
1/3 cup HERSHEY'S Cocoa
1/2 cup powdered sugar
1/2 cup (1 stick) butter or margarine, melted
3 packages (8 oz. each) cream cheese, softened
1 can (14 oz.) sweetened condensed milk
   (not evaporated milk)
3 eggs
2 teaspoons vanilla extract
4 sections (1/2 oz. each) HERSHEY'S Unsweetened
   Chocolate Premium Baking Bar, melted

1. Heat oven to 300°F.

2. Stir together vanilla wafer crumbs, cocoa and powdered sugar in medium bowl. Stir in melted butter until well blended. Press mixture firmly on bottom of 13×9×2-inch baking pan. Set aside.

3. Beat cream cheese in large bowl until fluffy. Gradually add sweetened condensed milk, beating until smooth. Add eggs and vanilla; mix well.

4. Pour half of batter evenly over prepared crust. Stir melted chocolate into remaining batter; drop by spoonfuls over vanilla batter. With metal spatula or knife, swirl gently through batter to marble.

5. Bake 45 to 50 minutes or until set. Cool in pan on wire rack. Refrigerate several hours until chilled. Cut into bars. Cover and refrigerate leftover bars.

HERSHEY'S

Chocolate Cranberry Bars

Makes 36 bars

- 2 cups vanilla wafer crumbs (about 60 wafers, crushed)
- ½ cup HERSHEY'S Cocoa
- 3 tablespoons sugar
- ⅔ cup cold butter, cut into pieces
- 1 can (14 oz.) sweetened condensed milk (not evaporated milk)
- 1 cup REESE'S Peanut Butter Chips
- 1⅓ cups (6-oz. pkg.) sweetened dried cranberries OR 1⅓ cups raisins
- 1 cup coarsely chopped walnuts

1. Heat oven to 350°F.

2. Stir together vanilla wafer crumbs, cocoa and sugar in medium bowl; cut in butter until crumbly. Press mixture evenly on bottom and ½ inch up sides of 13×9×2-inch baking pan. Pour sweetened condensed milk evenly over crumb mixture; sprinkle evenly with peanut butter chips and dried cranberries. Sprinkle nuts on top; press down firmly.

3. Bake 25 to 30 minutes or until lightly browned. Cool completely in pan on wire rack. Cover with foil; let stand several hours before cutting into bars and serving.

HERSHEY'S

Chocolate Streusel Bars

Makes 36 bars

1¾ cups all-purpose flour
1 cup sugar
¼ cup HERSHEY'S Cocoa
½ cup (1 stick) butter or margarine
1 egg
1 can (14 oz.) sweetened condensed milk
   (not evaporated milk)
2 cups (12-oz. pkg.) HERSHEY'S SPECIAL DARK
   Chocolate Chips or HERSHEY'S Semi-Sweet Chocolate
   Chips, divided
1 cup coarsely chopped nuts

1. Heat oven to 350°F. Grease 13×9×2-inch baking pan.

2. Stir together flour, sugar and cocoa in large bowl. Cut in butter until mixture resembles coarse crumbs. Add egg; mix well. Set aside 1½ cups mixture. Press remaining mixture onto bottom of prepared pan. Bake crust 10 minutes.

3. Meanwhile, place sweetened condensed milk and 1 cup chocolate chips in medium microwave-safe bowl; stir. Microwave at MEDIUM (50%) 1 to 1½ minutes or until chips are melted and mixture is smooth when stirred; pour over crust. Add nuts and remaining chips to reserved crumb mixture. Sprinkle over top.

4. Bake an additional 25 to 30 minutes or until center is almost set. Cool completely in pan on wire rack. Cut into bars.

HERSHEY'S

Chocolate Macaroon Bars

Makes 24 to 36 bars

1¼   cups graham cracker crumbs
⅓   cup sugar
¼   cup HERSHEY'S Cocoa
⅓   cup butter or margarine, melted
1   can (14 oz.) sweetened condensed milk
     (not evaporated milk)
2⅔   cups MOUNDS Sweetened Coconut Flakes
2   cups fresh white bread crumbs (about 5 slices)
2   eggs
2   teaspoons vanilla extract
1   cup HERSHEY'S Mini Chips Semi-Sweet Chocolate

1. Heat oven to 350°F.

2. Stir together graham cracker crumbs, sugar, cocoa and butter in large bowl; press firmly onto bottom of ungreased 13×9×2-inch baking pan.

3. Bake 10 minutes. Meanwhile, combine sweetened condensed milk, coconut, bread crumbs, eggs, vanilla and small chocolate chips in large bowl; stir until blended. Spoon over prepared crust, spreading evenly.

4. Bake 30 minutes or until lightly browned. Cool completely in pan on wire rack. Cut into bars. Cover and refrigerate leftover bars.

Cakes
& Cheesecakes

Brickle Bundt Cake

Makes 12 to 14 servings

1⅓ cups (8-oz. pkg.) HEATH BITS 'O BRICKLE Toffee Bits, divided

1¼ cups granulated sugar, divided

¼ cup chopped walnuts

1 teaspoon ground cinnamon

½ cup (1 stick) butter, softened

2 eggs

1¼ teaspoons vanilla extract, divided

2 cups all-purpose flour

1½ teaspoons baking powder

1 teaspoon baking soda

¼ teaspoon salt

1 container (8 oz.) dairy sour cream

¼ cup (½ stick) butter, melted

1 cup powdered sugar

1 to 3 tablespoons milk, divided

(recipe continued on page 114)

1. Heat oven to 325°F. Grease and flour 12-cup fluted tube pan or 10-inch tube pan. Set aside ¼ cup toffee bits for topping. Combine remaining toffee bits, ¼ cup granulated sugar, walnuts and cinnamon; set aside.

2. Beat remaining 1 cup granulated sugar and ½ cup butter in large bowl until fluffy. Add eggs and 1 teaspoon vanilla; beat well. Stir together flour, baking powder, baking soda and salt; gradually add to butter mixture, alternately with sour cream, beating until blended. Beat 3 minutes. Spoon one-third of the batter into prepared pan. Sprinkle with half of toffee mixture. Spoon half of remaining batter into pan. Top with remaining toffee mixture. Spoon remaining batter into pan. Pour melted butter over batter.

3. Bake 45 to 50 minutes or until wooden pick inserted in center comes out clean. Cool 10 minutes; remove from pan to wire rack. Cool completely.

4. Stir together powdered sugar, 1 tablespoon milk and remaining ¼ teaspoon vanilla extract. Stir in additional milk, 1 teaspoon at a time, until desired consistency; drizzle over cake. Sprinkle with remaining ¼ cup toffee bits.

Creamy Ambrosia Cheesecake

Makes 10 to 12 servings

1⅓	cups graham cracker crumbs
½	cup MOUNDS Sweetened Coconut Flakes
¼	cup (½ stick) melted butter or margarine
1¼	cups plus 2 tablespoons sugar, divided
1	can (11 oz.) mandarin orange segments
1	can (8 oz.) crushed pineapple in juice
3	packages (8 oz. each) cream cheese, softened
3	eggs

HERSHEY'S

2 cups (12-oz. pkg.) HERSHEY'S Premier White Chips
Tropical Fruit Sauce (recipe follows)
Additional MOUNDS Sweetened Coconut Flakes

1. Heat oven to 350°F. Stir graham cracker crumbs, coconut, melted butter and 2 tablespoons sugar in medium bowl. Press mixture firmly onto bottom of 9-inch springform pan. Bake 8 minutes; cool slightly. Drain oranges and pineapple, reserving juices. Chop oranges into small pieces.

2. Beat cream cheese in large bowl until fluffy. Add remaining 1¼ cups sugar; beat well. Add eggs; beat well. Stir in white chips, oranges and pineapple. Pour mixture over crust.

3. Bake 60 to 65 minutes or until center is almost set. Remove from oven to wire rack. With knife, loosen cake from side of pan. Cool completely; remove side of pan. Cover; refrigerate until cold. Garnish with additional coconut, if desired, and serve with Tropical Fruit Sauce. Cover and refrigerate leftovers.

Tropical Fruit Sauce

Makes about ¾ cup sauce

Juice drained from canned mandarin oranges
Juice drained from 1 can (8-oz.) crushed pineapple in juice
¼ **cup sugar**
1 **tablespoon cornstarch**
¼ **teaspoon orange extract or pineapple extract**

Combine fruit juices; pour 1 cup combined juice into medium saucepan and discard any remaining juices. Stir in sugar and cornstarch. Cook over medium heat, stirring constantly, until thickened. Remove from heat. Stir in orange extract or pineapple extract. Cool to room temperature before serving. Cover and refrigerate leftover sauce.

HERSHEY'S

HERSHEY'S HUGS and KISSES Candies Chocolate Cake

Makes 12 to 15 servings

- ¾ cup (1½ sticks) butter or margarine, softened
- 1¾ cups sugar
- 2 eggs
- 1 teaspoon vanilla extract
- 2 cups all-purpose flour
- ¾ cup HERSHEY'S Cocoa or HERSHEY'S SPECIAL DARK Cocoa
- 1¼ teaspoons baking soda
- ½ teaspoon salt
- 1⅓ cups water
- Cocoa Fudge Frosting (recipe follows)
- HERSHEY'S HUGS BRAND Chocolates and HERSHEY'S KISSES BRAND Milk Chocolates

1. Heat oven to 350°F. Grease and flour 13×9×2-inch baking pan.

2. Beat butter and sugar with electric mixer in large bowl until fluffy. Add eggs and vanilla; beat 1 minute on medium speed of mixer. Stir together flour, cocoa, baking soda and salt; add alternately with water to butter mixture, beating until well blended. Pour batter into prepared pan.

3. Bake 40 to 45 minutes or until wooden pick inserted in center comes out clean. Cool 10 minutes; remove from pan to wire rack. Cool completely. Frost with Cocoa Fudge Frosting. Remove wrappers from candies; garnish cake as desired with candies.

Cocoa Fudge Frosting

Makes about 2½ cups frosting

- ½ **cup (1 stick) butter or margarine**
- ½ **cup HERSHEY'S Cocoa or HERSHEY'S SPECIAL DARK Cocoa**
- 3⅔ **cups (1 lb.) powdered sugar**
- ⅓ **cup milk, heated**
- 1 **teaspoon vanilla extract**

Melt butter in small saucepan over low heat; stir in cocoa. Cook, stirring constantly, until mixture thickens slightly. Remove from heat; pour into small mixer bowl. Add powdered sugar alternately with warm milk, beating to spreading consistency. Stir in vanilla. Spread frosting while warm.

HERSHEY'S

Dandy Cake

Makes 20 to 24 servings

  1 **cup water**
  1 **cup (2 sticks) butter or margarine**
 1/3 **cup HERSHEY'S Cocoa**
  2 **cups all-purpose flour**
  2 **cups sugar**
  1 **teaspoon baking soda**
 1/2 **teaspoon salt**
  3 **eggs**
 3/4 **cup dairy sour cream**
 3/4 **cup REESE'S Creamy Peanut Butter**
     CHOCOLATE TOPPING (recipe follows)

1. Heat oven to 350°F. Grease and flour 15½×10½×1-inch jelly-roll pan.

2. Combine water, butter and cocoa in small saucepan. Cook over medium heat, stirring occasionally, until mixture boils; boil and stir 1 minute. Remove from heat; set aside.

3. Stir together flour, sugar, baking soda and salt in large bowl. Add eggs and sour cream; beat until well blended. Add cocoa mixture; beat just until blended (batter will be thin). Pour into prepared pan.

4. Bake 25 to 30 minutes or until wooden pick inserted in center comes out clean. Do not remove cake from pan; spread peanut butter over warm cake. Cool completely in pan on wire rack. Prepare CHOCOLATE TOPPING; carefully spread over top, covering peanut butter. Allow topping to set; cut into squares.

HERSHEY'S

CHOCOLATE TOPPING: Place 2 cups (12-oz. pkg.) HERSHEY'S SPECIAL DARK Chocolate Chips or HERSHEY'S Semi-Sweet Chocolate Chips and 2 tablespoons shortening (do not use butter, margarine, spread or oil) in small microwave-safe bowl. Microwave at MEDIUM (50%) 1½ minutes; stir. If necessary, microwave at MEDIUM an additional 15 seconds at a time, stirring after each heating, just until chips are melted when stirred.

HERSHEY'S

HERSHEY'S "Especially Dark" Chocolate Cake

Makes 10 to 12 servings

2	cups sugar
1¾	cups all-purpose flour
¾	cup HERSHEY'S SPECIAL DARK Cocoa
1½	teaspoons baking powder
1½	teaspoons baking soda
1	teaspoon salt
2	eggs
1	cup milk
½	cup vegetable oil
2	teaspoons vanilla extract
1	cup boiling water
	"Especially Dark" Chocolate Frosting (recipe follows)

1. Heat oven to 350°F. Grease and flour two 9-inch round baking pans.

2. Stir together sugar, flour, cocoa, baking powder, baking soda and salt in large bowl. Add eggs, milk, oil and vanilla; beat with electric mixer on medium speed for 2 minutes. Stir in boiling water (batter will be thin). Pour batter into prepared pans.

3. Bake 30 to 35 minutes or until wooden pick inserted in center comes out clean. Cool 10 minutes; remove from pans to wire racks. Cool completely. Frost with "Especially Dark" Chocolate Frosting.

"Especially Dark" Chocolate Frosting

Makes 2 cups frosting

- ½ cup (1 stick) butter or margarine
- ⅔ cup HERSHEY'S SPECIAL DARK Cocoa
- 3 cups powdered sugar
- ⅓ cup milk
- 1 teaspoon vanilla extract

Melt butter. Stir in cocoa. Alternately add powdered sugar and milk, beating to spreading consistency. Add small amount additional milk, if needed. Stir in vanilla.

HERSHEY'S

Fiesta Fantasy Cake

Makes 16 to 20 servings

2 cups sifted cake flour or 1¾ cups sifted all-purpose flour

½ cup HERSHEY'S SPECIAL DARK Cocoa or HERSHEY'S Cocoa

2 teaspoons baking soda

¼ teaspoon salt

2 cups packed light brown sugar

⅔ cup butter, softened

3 eggs

1 tablespoon coffee liqueur or strong coffee

½ teaspoon vanilla extract

1 container (8 oz.) dairy sour cream

¾ cup boiling water

Chocolate Mousse (recipe follows)

Chocolate Frosting (recipe follows)

1. Heat oven to 350°F. Grease and flour two 9-inch round cake pans. Combine flour, cocoa, baking soda and salt. Set aside.

2. Beat brown sugar and butter with electric mixer on low or medium speed in large bowl until combined. Add eggs, one at a time, beating well after each addition. Beat in coffee liqueur or coffee and vanilla. Add flour mixture and sour cream alternately to sugar mixture, beating after each addition just until combined. Stir in boiling water until blended. Pour into prepared pans.

HERSHEY'S

3. Bake 30 to 35 minutes or until wooden pick inserted near centers comes out clean. Cool in pans on wire racks 10 minutes; remove from pans to wire racks. Cool completely.

4. Prepare Chocolate Mousse. Split each cake layer horizontally to make four layers total. Place one layer on serving plate; spread with one-third (about 1 cup) Chocolate Mousse. Repeat layering with two of the remaining layers and remaining mousse. Place remaining cake layer on top. Prepare Chocolate Frosting; frost cake top and sides. Cover; refrigerate at least 2 hours before serving.

Chocolate Mousse

Makes about 3 cups mousse

- 2 **cups (12-oz. pkg.) HERSHEY'S SPECIAL DARK Chocolate Chips or HERSHEY'S Semi-Sweet Chocolate Chips**
- 1⅓ **cup whipping cream, divided**
- 3 **tablespoons sugar**
- ¼ **cup coffee liqueur or strong coffee**
- 1 **tablespoon vanilla extract**

Place chocolate chips in food processor bowl; process until finely ground. Mix ⅓ cup whipping cream and granulated sugar in 1-quart saucepan. Cook over medium heat, stirring constantly, until sugar is dissolved and mixture is just boiling. With food processor running, pour hot cream through feed tube, processing 10 to 20 seconds or until chocolate is completely melted. Scrape side of food processor bowl. Add liqueur or strong coffee and vanilla extract; process 10 to 20 seconds or until smooth. Pour into large bowl;

(recipe continued on page 124)

cool about 10 minutes or until mixture is room temperature. Beat remaining 1 cup whipping cream in chilled medium bowl with electric mixer on high speed just until soft peaks form. Fold whipped cream into chocolate mixture. Cover; refrigerate at least 30 minutes.

Chocolate Frosting

Makes about 3 cups frosting

- 1½ **cups sifted powdered sugar**
- ⅔ **cup HERSHEY'S SPECIAL DARK Cocoa**
- 1½ **cups whipping cream**
- 1 **teaspoon vanilla extract**
- 3 **to 4 tablespoons milk**

Stir together powdered sugar and cocoa in medium mixer bowl. Stir in whipping cream and vanilla. Beat on low speed of mixer until stiff peaks form, scraping side of bowl constantly. (Mixture will be very stiff.) By hand, stir in milk 1 tablespoon at a time to make desired consistency.

HERSHEY'S

Chocolate & Peanut Butter Fudge Cheesecake

Makes 10 to 12 servings

1½ cups vanilla wafer crumbs (about 45 wafers, crushed)

½ cup powdered sugar

¼ cup HERSHEY'S Cocoa

⅓ cup butter or margarine, melted

3 packages (8 oz. each) cream cheese, softened

¾ cup granulated sugar

3 eggs

⅓ cup dairy sour cream

3 tablespoons all-purpose flour

1 teaspoon vanilla extract

¼ teaspoon salt

1 cup HERSHEY'S SPECIAL DARK Chocolate Chips or HERSHEY'S Semi-Sweet Chocolate Chips, melted

1 cup REESE'S Peanut Butter Chips, melted

HERSHEY'S Fudge Topping (optional)

Sweetened whipped cream (optional)

1. Heat oven to 350°F. Combine vanilla wafer crumbs, powdered sugar, cocoa and melted butter in medium bowl. Press onto bottom and 1 inch up side of 9-inch springform pan. Bake 8 minutes; cool.

2. Beat cream cheese and sugar in large bowl until smooth. Add eggs, sour cream, flour, vanilla and salt; beat until well blended.

3. Place half of batter in separate bowl. Stir melted chocolate into one bowl of cream cheese mixture and melted peanut butter chips into the other. Spread chocolate mixture in prepared crust. Gently spread peanut butter mixture over chocolate mixture. Do not stir.

HERSHEY'S

4. Bake 50 to 55 minutes or until center is almost set. (For less cracking of cheesecake surface, bake in water bath.) Remove from oven to wire rack. With knife, loosen cake from side of pan. Cool completely; remove side of pan. Cover; refrigerate.

5. To serve, drizzle each slice with fudge topping and top with whipped cream, if desired. Cover; refrigerate leftover cheesecake.

HERSHEY'S

Macadamia
Nuts

White Chip and Macadamia Nut Coffeecake

Makes 12 to 16 servings

    Crumb Topping (recipe follows)
  6 tablespoons butter or margarine, softened
 ¾ cup granulated sugar
 ¾ cup packed light brown sugar
  2 cups all-purpose flour
  2 teaspoons baking powder
 ½ teaspoon ground cinnamon
1¼ cups milk
  1 egg
  1 teaspoon vanilla extract
    White Drizzle (recipe follows)

1. Heat oven to 350°F. Grease and flour 13×9×2-inch baking pan. Prepare Crumb Topping; set aside.

(recipe continued on page 130)

2. Beat butter, granulated sugar and brown sugar until well blended. Stir together flour, baking powder and cinnamon; beat into butter mixture. Gradually add milk, egg and vanilla, beating until thoroughly blended. Pour half batter into prepared pan; top with half Crumb Topping. Gently spread remaining batter over topping. Sprinkle remaining topping over batter.

3. Bake 30 to 35 minutes or until wooden pick inserted into center comes out clean. Cool completely.

4. Prepare White Drizzle; drizzle over cake.

CRUMB TOPPING: Combine ⅔ cup packed light brown sugar, ½ cup all-purpose flour, 6 tablespoons firm butter or margarine and 1⅓ cups (8-oz. pkg.) HERSHEY'S Premier White Chips and Macadamia Nuts in medium bowl. Mix until crumbly.

WHITE DRIZZLE: Beat together ¾ cup powdered sugar, 2 to 3 teaspoons milk, 1 teaspoon softened butter and ¼ teaspoon vanilla extract. If necessary, stir in additional milk ½ teaspoon at a time until desired consistency.

Chip and Macadamia Nut Cookie Cups

Makes 5 dozen cookie cups

- 1 cup (2 sticks) butter or margarine, softened
- 2 packages (3 oz. each) cream cheese, softened
- 2 cups all-purpose flour
- ½ cup sugar

HERSHEY'S

1⅓ cups (8-oz. pkg.) HERSHEY'S SPECIAL DARK Chips
     and Macadamia Nuts

1   cup MOUNDS Sweetened Coconut Flakes

2   eggs

1   can (14 oz.) sweetened condensed milk (not
     evaporated milk)

2   tablespoons light corn syrup

1   teaspoon vanilla extract

½   teaspoon coconut extract

⅛   teaspoon salt

1. Beat butter and cream cheese in large bowl until well blended. Gradually add flour and sugar, beating until blended. If necessary, cover and refrigerate dough until easy to handle.

2. Divide dough into 5 equal parts. Shape each part into 12 smooth balls. Place each ball in small muffin cup (1¾ inches diameter); press evenly on bottom and up side of each cup.

3. Heat oven to 375°F. Stir together chip mixture and coconut; divide evenly into prepared cups. Beat eggs in small bowl. Add sweetened condensed milk, corn syrup, vanilla, coconut extract and salt; mix well. Evenly divide milk mixture into the cups.

4. Bake 18 to 20 minutes or until tops are puffed and turn light golden brown. Cool completely in pan on wire rack. Remove from pan using small metal spatula or sharp knife. Store tightly covered at room temperature.

HERSHEY'S

HERSHEY'S SPECIAL DARK Chips
and Macadamia Nut Cookies

Makes 3½ dozen cookies

6	tablespoons butter, softened
⅓	cup butter flavored shortening
½	cup packed light brown sugar
⅓	cup granulated sugar
1	egg
1½	teaspoons vanilla extract
1⅓	cups all-purpose flour
½	teaspoon baking soda
½	teaspoon salt
1⅓	cups (8-oz. pkg.) HERSHEY'S SPECIAL DARK Chips and Macadamia Nuts

1. Heat oven to 350°F.

2. Beat butter and shortening in large bowl until well blended. Add brown sugar and granulated sugar; beat thoroughly. Add egg and vanilla, beating until well blended. Stir together flour, baking soda and salt; gradually beat into butter mixture. Stir in baking pieces. Drop by rounded teaspoons onto ungreased cookie sheet.

3. Bake 10 to 12 minutes or until edges are lightly browned. Cool slightly; transfer to wire rack. Cool completely.

WHITE CHIPS AND MACADAMIA PIECES VARIATION: Substitute 1⅓ cups (8-oz. pkg.) HERSHEY'S Premier White Chips and Macadamia Nuts for HERSHEY'S SPECIAL DARK Chips and Macadamia Nuts. Prepare as directed above.

CHOCOLATE COOKIE VARIATION: Decrease flour to 1 cup; add ⅓ cup HERSHEY'S Cocoa or HERSHEY'S SPECIAL DARK Cocoa.

HERSHEY'S

Chocolate Macadamia Truffle Mousse Pie

Makes 6 to 8 servings

9-inch baked and cooled pastry crust or packaged crumb crust (6 oz.)

1⅓ cups (8-oz. pkg.) HERSHEY'S SPECIAL DARK Chips and Macadamia Nuts, divided

3 tablespoons plus 1 cup (½ pint) cold whipping cream

1 teaspoon unflavored gelatin

1 tablespoon cold water

2 tablespoons boiling water

½ cup sugar

¼ cup HERSHEY'S Cocoa

1 teaspoon vanilla extract

Sweetened whipped cream or whipped topping

1. Set aside ⅓ cup chip and nut mixture. Place remaining mixture and 3 tablespoons whipping cream in medium microwave-safe bowl. Microwave at MEDIUM (50%) 1 minute; stir. If necessary, microwave at MEDIUM an additional 15 seconds at a time, stirring after each heating, until chips are melted when stirred. Spread mixture on bottom of prepared crust. Refrigerate while preparing next steps.

2. Sprinkle gelatin over cold water; let stand 1 minute to soften. Add boiling water; stir until gelatin is completely dissolved and mixture is clear. Cool slightly, about 5 minutes.

3. Meanwhile, stir together sugar and cocoa in small mixing bowl; add remaining 1 cup whipping cream and vanilla. Beat on medium speed of electric mixer, scraping bottom of bowl occasionally, until stiff. Pour in gelatin mixture, beating until just well blended.

HERSHEY'S

4. Carefully spread over chocolate layer in crust. Cover; refrigerate several hours or until firm. Garnish with whipped cream and remaining chip and nut mixture.

HERSHEY'S

HERSHEY'S SPECIAL DARK
and Macadamia Toffee Crunch

Makes 1 pound candy

1⅓ **cups (8-oz. pkg.) HERSHEY'S SPECIAL DARK Chips and Macadamia Nuts, divided**

¾ **cup (1½ sticks) butter**

¾ **cup sugar**

3 **tablespoons light corn syrup**

1. Line 8- or 9-inch square or round pan with foil, extending foil over edges of pan; butter foil. Reserve 2 tablespoons chocolate chip and nut mixture; sprinkle remaining chip mixture over bottom of prepared pan.

2. Combine butter, sugar and corn syrup in heavy medium saucepan; cook over low heat, stirring constantly, until butter is melted and sugar is dissolved. Increase heat to medium; cook, stirring constantly, until mixture boils. Cook and stir until mixture turns a light caramel color (about 15 minutes).

3. Immediately pour mixture over chip and nut mixture in pan, spreading evenly. Sprinkle reserved chip mixture over surface. Cool. Refrigerate until chocolate is firm. Remove from pan; peel off foil. Break into pieces. Store tightly covered in cool, dry place.

WHITE CHIP AND MACADAMIA TOFFEE CRUNCH: Substitute 1⅓ cups (8-oz. pkg.) HERSHEY'S Premier White Chips and Macadamia Nuts for HERSHEY'S SPECIAL DARK Chips and Macadamia Nuts. Proceed as above.

HERSHEY'S

HERSHEY'S Premier White Chips and Macadamia Nut Fudge

Makes about 5 dozen pieces (about 2¼ pounds) candy

1¾ cups sugar
1 jar (7 oz.) marshmallow crème
¾ cup evaporated milk
¼ cup (½ stick) butter
2⅔ cups (two 8-oz. pkgs.) HERSHEY'S Premier White Chips and Macadamia Nuts
1 teaspoon vanilla extract

1. Line 8-inch square pan with foil, extending foil over edges of pan.

2. Combine sugar, marshmallow crème, evaporated milk and butter in heavy 3-quart saucepan. Cook over medium heat, stirring constantly, until mixture comes to a full boil; boil and stir 5 minutes.

3. Remove from heat. Gradually stir in chips and nuts, stirring until chips are melted. Stir in vanilla. Pour into prepared pan; cool until set.

4. Remove from pan; place on cutting board. Peel off foil. Cut into squares. Store tightly covered in cool, dry place.

SPECIAL DARK VARIATION: Substitute 2⅔ cups (two 8-oz. pkgs.) HERSHEY'S SPECIAL DARK Chips and Macadamia Nuts for HERSHEY'S Premier White Chips and Macadamia Nuts. Prepare as directed above.

NOTE: For best results, do not double this recipe.

HERSHEY'S

HERSHEY'S SPECIAL DARK
Chips and Macadamia Nut Shortbread Wedges

Makes 2 dozen cookies

- 1 cup (2 sticks) butter (no substitutes), softened
- ½ cup sugar
- 2½ cups all-purpose flour
- 1 tablespoon vanilla extract
- 1⅓ cups (8-oz. pkg.) HERSHEY'S SPECIAL DARK Chips and Macadamia Nuts

1. Heat oven to 350°F. Grease cookie sheet or line with parchment paper.

2. Beat butter and sugar in large bowl until fluffy. Beat in flour and vanilla and continue beating until dough forms pea-sized crumbs. Stir in chips and macadamia nuts. Shape mixture into ball; divide into two smaller equal balls.

3. Place one dough ball at each end of prepared cookie sheet; flatten each into circle about ½ inch thick. With knife cut each circle into 12 wedges. Do not separate wedges.

4. Bake 20 to 25 minutes or until edges are golden brown and center is set. Cool 10 minutes; recut wedges.

HERSHEY'S

Tropical Paradise Scones

Makes 24 scones

3¼ cups all-purpose flour

½ cup sugar

1 tablespoon plus 1 teaspoon baking powder

¼ teaspoon salt

1 cup MOUNDS Sweetened Coconut Flakes

1⅓ cups (8-oz. pkg.) HERSHEY'S White Chips and Macadamia Nuts

2 cups chilled whipping cream

2 tablespoons fresh lime juice

2 to 3 teaspoons freshly grated lime peel

2 tablespoons butter, melted

Additional sugar

1. Heat oven to 375°F. Lightly grease 2 baking sheets.

2. Stir together flour, ½ cup sugar, baking powder and salt in large bowl. Stir in coconut and white chips and macadamia nuts.

3. Stir whipping cream, lime juice and lime peel into flour mixture, stirring just until ingredients are moistened.

4. Turn mixture out onto lightly floured surface. Knead gently until soft dough forms (about 2 minutes). Divide dough into three equal balls. One ball at a time, flatten into 7-inch circle; cut into 8 triangles. Transfer triangles to prepared baking sheets, spacing 2 inches apart. Brush with melted butter and sprinkle with additional sugar.

5. Bake 15 to 20 minutes or until lightly browned. Serve warm or cool.

HERSHEY'S
Cookies

HERSHEY'S Mini KISSES
Milk Chocolate Peanut Butter
Cookies

Makes 18 cookies

- ¼ cup (½ stick) butter or margarine, softened
- ¼ cup REESE'S Creamy Peanut Butter
- ¼ cup granulated sugar
- ¼ cup packed light brown sugar
- 1 egg
- ½ teaspoon vanilla extract
- ⅔ cup all-purpose flour
- ¼ teaspoon baking soda
- ⅛ teaspoon salt
- 1¾ cups (10-oz. pkg.) HERSHEY'S Mini KISSES BRAND Milk Chocolates

1. Heat oven to 350°F. Lightly grease cookie sheet.

(recipe continued on page 144)

2. Beat butter and peanut butter in large bowl on medium speed of electric mixer until creamy. Gradually add granulated sugar and brown sugar, beating until well mixed. Add egg and vanilla; beat until light and fluffy. Stir together flour, baking soda and salt; add to butter mixture, beating until well blended. Stir in chocolates. Drop batter by rounded tablespoons onto prepared cookie sheet.

3. Bake 10 to 12 minutes or until lightly browned. Cool slightly; remove from cookie sheet to wire rack. Cool completely.

Chewy Chocolate Macaroons

Makes 4 dozen cookies

5⅓ cups MOUNDS Sweetened Coconut Flakes
½ cup HERSHEY'S Cocoa
1 can (14 oz.) sweetened condensed milk (not evaporated milk)
2 teaspoons vanilla extract
About 24 red candied cherries, halved

1. Heat oven to 350°F. Generously grease cookie sheet.

2. Stir together coconut and cocoa in large bowl; stir in sweetened condensed milk and vanilla until well blended. Drop by rounded teaspoons onto prepared cookie sheet. Press cherry half into center of each cookie.

3. Bake 8 to 10 minutes or until almost set. Immediately remove from cookie sheet to wire rack. Cool completely. Store loosely covered at room temperature.

HERSHEY'S

Chewy Brownie Cookies

Makes about 3 dozen cookies

⅔ cup shortening

1½ cups packed light brown sugar

1 tablespoon water

1 teaspoon vanilla extract

2 eggs

1½ cups all-purpose flour

⅓ cup HERSHEY'S Cocoa or HERSHEY'S SPECIAL DARK Cocoa

½ teaspoon salt

¼ teaspoon baking soda

2 cups (12-oz. pkg.) HERSHEY'S SPECIAL DARK Chocolate Chips or HERSHEY'S Semi-Sweet Chocolate Chips

¼ cup chopped walnuts (optional)

1. Heat oven to 375°F.

2. Beat shortening, brown sugar, water and vanilla in large bowl on medium speed of mixer until well blended. Add eggs; beat well.

3. Stir together flour, cocoa, salt and baking soda. Gradually add to sugar mixture, beating on low speed just until blended. Stir in chocolate chips. Drop by rounded tablespoons 2 inches apart onto ungreased cookie sheet. Sprinkle chopped walnuts on each cookie, pressing down lightly.

4. Bake 7 to 9 minutes or until cookies are set. Cookies will appear soft and moist. Do not overbake. Cool 2 minutes; remove from cookie sheet to wire rack. Cool completely.

HERSHEY'S

Chocolate Chip & Toffee Bits Cookies

Makes 4 dozen cookies

2¼ cups all-purpose flour

1 teaspoon baking soda

½ teaspoon salt

¾ cup (1½ sticks) butter or margarine, softened

¾ cup granulated sugar

¾ cup packed light brown sugar

1 teaspoon vanilla extract

2 eggs

1 cup HEATH BITS 'O BRICKLE Toffee Bits

1 cup HERSHEY'S SPECIAL DARK Chocolate Chips or HERSHEY'S Semi-Sweet Chocolate Chips

1. Heat oven to 375°F.

2. Stir together flour, baking soda and salt. Beat butter, granulated sugar, brown sugar and vanilla in large bowl until well blended. Add eggs; beat well. Gradually add flour mixture, beating well. Stir in toffee bits and chocolate chips. Drop by rounded teaspoons onto ungreased cookie sheet.

3. Bake 8 to 10 minutes or until lightly browned. Cool slightly; remove from cookie sheet to wire rack. Cool completely.

HERSHEY'S

Double Peanut Butter and Milk Chocolate Chip Cookies

Makes about 3 dozen cookies

½ **cup (1 stick) butter or margarine, softened**
¾ **cup sugar**
⅓ **cup REESE'S Creamy Peanut Butter**
1 **egg**
½ **teaspoon vanilla extract**
1¼ **cups all-purpose flour**
½ **teaspoon baking soda**
¼ **teaspoon salt**
1 **cup HERSHEY'S Milk Chocolate Chips**
1 **cup REESE'S Peanut Butter Chips**

1. Heat oven to 350°F.

2. Beat butter, sugar and peanut butter in medium bowl until creamy. Add egg and vanilla; beat well. Stir together flour, baking soda and salt; add to peanut butter mixture, blending well. Stir in milk chocolate chips and peanut butter chips. Drop by rounded teaspoons onto ungreased cookie sheets.

3. Bake 12 to 14 minutes or until light golden brown around the edges. Cool 1 minute on cookie sheet. Remove to wire rack; cool completely.

4 very good regular Snickerdoodles probably better

HERSHEY'S

Toffee Studded Snickerdoodles

Makes about 5 dozen cookies

½ **cup (1 stick) butter or margarine, softened**
½ **cup shortening**
1 **cup plus 3 tablespoons sugar, divided**
2 **eggs**
2¾ **cups all-purpose flour**
2 **teaspoons cream of tartar**
1 **teaspoon baking soda**
¼ **teaspoon salt**
1⅓ **cups (8-oz. pkg.) HEATH BITS 'O BRICKLE Toffee Bits**
1 **teaspoon ground cinnamon**

1. Heat oven to 400°F.

2. Beat butter, shortening and 1 cup sugar in large bowl until fluffy. Add eggs; beat thoroughly. Stir together flour, cream of tartar, baking soda and salt; gradually add to butter mixture, beating until well blended. Stir in toffee bits.

3. Stir together remaining 3 tablespoons sugar and cinnamon. Shape dough into 1¼-inch balls; roll in sugar-cinnamon mixture. Place on ungreased cookie sheet.

4. Bake 9 to 11 minutes or until lightly browned around edges. Cool 1 minute; remove from cookie sheet to wire rack. Cool completely.

HERSHEY'S

Chocolate Blossoms Made with HERSHEY'S Mini KISSES Milk Chocolates

Makes about 4 dozen cookies

1   cup (2 sticks) butter or margarine, softened
1½ cups sugar
2   eggs
2   teaspoons vanilla extract
2   cups all-purpose flour
½   cup HERSHEY'S Cocoa
½   teaspoon salt
    Additional sugar
1¾ cups (10-oz. pkg.) HERSHEY'S Mini KISSES BRAND
    Milk Chocolates

1. Beat butter, 1½ cups sugar, eggs and vanilla in large bowl until fluffy. Combine flour, cocoa and salt; gradually add to butter mixture, beating until well blended. Refrigerate dough about 1 hour or until firm enough to handle.

2. Heat oven to 350°F. Shape dough into 1⅛-inch balls; roll in sugar. Place on ungreased cookie sheet.

3. Bake 8 to 10 minutes or until set. Remove from oven. Place 3 chocolate pieces on each cookie, pressing down lightly. Remove from cookie sheet to wire rack. Cool completely.

HERSHEY'S

HERSHEY'S CHOCOLATETOWN Chip Cookies

Makes 5 dozen cookies

1 cup shortening OR ¾ cup (1½ sticks) butter or margarine
1 cup packed light brown sugar
½ cup granulated sugar
1 teaspoon vanilla extract
2 eggs
2¼ cups all-purpose flour
1 teaspoon baking soda
1 teaspoon salt
2 cups (11½-oz. pkg.) HERSHEY'S Milk Chocolate Chips
1 cup chopped nuts (optional)

1. Heat oven to 375°F.

2. Beat shortening or butter, brown sugar, granulated sugar and vanilla in large bowl until fluffy. Add eggs; beat well.

3. Stir together flour, baking soda and salt; add to sugar mixture, beating until well blended. Stir in chips and nuts, if desired. Drop by teaspoons onto ungreased cookie sheet.

4. Bake 8 to 10 minutes or until lightly browned. Cool slightly; remove from cookie sheet to wire rack. Cool completely.

HERSHEY'S

SPECIAL DARK Tiger Cookies

Makes about 4 dozen cookies

1½   cups granulated sugar

½   cup vegetable oil

½   cup HERSHEY'S SPECIAL DARK Cocoa or HERSHEY'S Cocoa

3   eggs

1½   teaspoons vanilla extract

1¾   cups all-purpose flour

1½   teaspoons baking powder

½   teaspoon salt

Powdered sugar

48   HERSHEY'S KISSES BRAND SPECIAL DARK Chocolates or HERSHEY'S KISSES BRAND Milk Chocolates, unwrapped, (optional)

1. Stir together granulated sugar and oil in large bowl; add cocoa, beating until well blended. Beat in eggs and vanilla. Stir together flour, baking powder and salt; gradually add to cocoa mixture, beating well.

2. Cover; refrigerate until dough is firm enough to handle, at least 6 hours.

3. Heat oven to 350°F. Grease cookie sheet. Shape dough into 1-inch balls (dough will still be sticky); roll in powdered sugar to coat. Place about 2 inches apart on prepared cookie sheet.

4. Bake 11 to 13 minutes or until almost no indentation remains when touched lightly and tops are cracked. Immediately press chocolate piece into center of each cookie, if desired. Cool slightly. Transfer to wire rack. Cool completely.

HERSHEY'S

Jolly Peanut Butter Gingerbread Cookies

Makes about 6 dozen cookies

- 1²/₃ cups (10-oz. pkg.) REESE'S Peanut Butter Chips
- ¾ cup (1½ sticks) butter or margarine, softened
- 1 cup packed light brown sugar
- 1 cup dark corn syrup
- 2 eggs
- 5 cups all-purpose flour
- 1 teaspoon baking soda
- ½ teaspoon ground cinnamon
- ¼ teaspoon ground ginger
- ¼ teaspoon salt

1. Place peanut butter chips in small microwave-safe bowl. Microwave at MEDIUM (50%) 1 to 2 minutes or until chips are melted when stirred.

2. Beat melted peanut butter chips and butter in large bowl until well blended. Add brown sugar, corn syrup and eggs; beat until fluffy. Stir together flour, baking soda, cinnamon, ginger and salt. Add half of flour mixture to butter mixture; beat on low speed of mixer until smooth. With wooden spoon, stir in remaining flour mixture until well blended. Divide into thirds; wrap each in plastic wrap. Refrigerate until dough is firm enough to roll, at least 1 hour.

3. Heat oven to 325°F. On lightly floured surface, roll 1 dough portion at a time to ⅛-inch thickness; cut into holiday shapes with floured cookie cutters. Place on ungreased cookie sheet.

4. Bake 10 to 12 minutes or until set and lightly browned. Cool slightly; remove from cookie sheet to wire rack. Cool completely. Frost and decorate as desired.

HERSHEY'S

Peanut Butter and Chips Cookies

Makes 5½ dozen cookies

  1 cup (2 sticks) butter or margarine, softened
  1 cup sugar
  1 cup REESE'S Creamy Peanut Butter
 ¼ cup light corn syrup
  1 egg
  1 teaspoon vanilla extract
  2 cups all-purpose flour
  1 teaspoon baking soda
 ¼ teaspoon salt
1⅔ cups (10-oz. pkg.) REESE'S Peanut Butter Chips or
     2 cups (11½-oz. pkg.) HERSHEY'S Milk Chocolate
     Chips

1. Beat butter and sugar in large bowl until light and fluffy. Add peanut butter, corn syrup, egg and vanilla; beat well. Stir together flour, baking soda and salt; add to peanut butter mixture, beating until well blended. Stir in chips. Refrigerate 1 hour or until firm enough to handle.

2. Heat oven to 350°F. Shape dough into 1-inch balls. Place on ungreased cookie sheet.

3. Bake 9 to 11 minutes or until light brown around edges. Cool slightly; remove from cookie sheet to wire rack. Cool completely.

HERSHEY'S

Cookies Made with
HERSHEY'S SPECIAL DARK
Chocolate Chips

Makes about 3½ dozen cookies

  6 tablespoons butter, softened
 ⅓ cup butter flavored shortening
 ½ cup packed light brown sugar
 ⅓ cup granulated sugar
  1 egg
1½ teaspoons vanilla extract
1¼ cups all-purpose flour
 ½ teaspoon baking soda
 ½ teaspoon salt
  2 cups (12-oz. pkg.) HERSHEY'S SPECIAL DARK
      Chocolate Chips
 ¾ cup chopped nuts, optional

1. Heat oven to 350°F.

2. Beat butter and shortening in large bowl until well blended. Add brown sugar and granulated sugar; beat thoroughly. Add egg and vanilla, beating until well blended. Stir together flour, baking soda and salt; gradually beat into butter mixture. Stir in chocolate chips and nuts, if desired. Drop by rounded teaspoons onto ungreased cookie sheet.

3. Bake 10 to 12 minutes or until lightly browned. Cool slightly; remove from cookie sheet to wire rack. Cool completely.

HERSHEY'S

Cinnamon Chip Apple Cookies

Makes about 4 dozen cookies

¾ cup (1½ sticks) butter or margarine, softened
1 cup packed light brown sugar
1 egg
1 tablespoon apple juice or water
½ teaspoon vanilla extract
1½ cups all-purpose flour
1 teaspoon baking powder
½ teaspoon baking soda
¼ teaspoon salt
1½ cups quick-cooking oats
1⅔ cups (10-oz. pkg.) HERSHEY'S Cinnamon Chips
1 cup chopped, peeled apple
½ cup raisins

1. Heat oven to 350°F. Lightly grease cookie sheet.

2. Beat butter, brown sugar, egg, apple juice and vanilla in large bowl until creamy. Stir together flour, baking powder, baking soda and salt. Add to butter mixture; beat until blended. Stir in oats. Add cinnamon chips, apple and raisins; stir until blended. Drop by teaspoons onto prepared cookie sheet.

3. Bake 10 minutes or until edges are lightly browned. Cool 1 minute; remove from cookie sheet to wire rack. Cool completely.

HERSHEY'S

Chewy Chocolate Oatmeal Cookies

Makes 4 to 5 dozen cookies

½ cup (1 stick) butter or margarine, melted
½ cup HERSHEY'S Cocoa
1 can (14 oz.) sweetened condensed milk (not evaporated milk)
2 eggs, beaten
2 teaspoons vanilla extract
1½ cups quick-cooking rolled oats
1 cup all-purpose biscuit baking mix
¼ teaspoon salt
2 cups (12-oz. pkg.) HERSHEY'S Premier White Chips
1⅔ cups (10-oz. pkg.) REESE'S Peanut Butter Chips

1. Heat oven to 350°F. Lightly grease cookie sheet.

2. Stir together butter and cocoa in large bowl until mixture is smooth. Stir in sweetened condensed milk, eggs, vanilla extract, oats, baking mix, salt, white chips and peanut butter chips until well blended. Let batter rest 10 minutes; drop by heaping teaspoons onto prepared cookie sheet.

3. Bake 7 to 9 minutes or until cookies are set and tops begin to dry (do not overbake). Cool 5 minutes; remove from cookie sheet to wire rack. Cool completely. Store in airtight container.

VARIATION: Omit 1⅔ cups (10-oz. pkg.) chips; use only 1 package of desired flavor chips.

HERSHEY'S

Pies

& Desserts

Easy Chocolate Cheese Pie

Makes 6 to 8 servings

4 sections (½ oz. each) HERSHEY'S Unsweetened Chocolate Premium Baking Bar, broken into pieces

¼ cup (½ stick) butter or margarine, softened

¾ cup sugar

1 package (3 oz.) cream cheese, softened

1 teaspoon milk

2 cups frozen whipped topping, thawed

1 packaged crumb crust (6 oz.)

Additional whipped topping (optional)

1. Place chocolate in small microwave-safe bowl. Microwave at MEDIUM (50%) 1 to 1½ minutes or until chocolate is melted and smooth when stirred.

2. Beat butter, sugar, cream cheese and milk in medium bowl until well blended and smooth; fold in melted chocolate.

3. Fold in 2 cups whipped topping; spoon into crust. Cover; refrigerate until firm, about 3 hours. Garnish with additional whipped topping, if desired.

HERSHEY'S

Chocolate Cups with Lemon Cream

Makes 6 cookie cups

½ **cup sugar**

¼ **cup plus 2 tablespoons all-purpose flour**

2 **tablespoons HERSHEY'S Cocoa**

2 **egg whites**

¼ **cup (½ stick) butter or margarine, melted**

¾ **cup HERSHEY'S SPECIAL DARK Chocolate Chips or HERSHEY'S Semi-Sweet Chocolate Chips**

1 **teaspoon shortening (not butter, margarine, spread or oil)**

1 **package (4-serving size) instant lemon pudding and pie filling mix**

1 **cup milk**

⅛ **teaspoon lemon extract**

1½ **cups thawed non-dairy whipped topping**
    Freshly shredded lemon peel (optional)

1. Heat oven to 400°F. Grease and flour cookie sheet.

2. Stir together sugar, flour and cocoa in small bowl. Add egg whites and butter; beat until smooth. Drop teaspoons of mixture onto prepared cookie sheet; spread into thin 5-inch circles with back of spoon.

3. Bake 6 to 7 minutes or until set. Immediately remove from cookie sheet; place top-side down, over bottom of inverted juice glasses. Mold to give wavy edges. (If chocolate cup cracks, gently press together with fingers.) Let stand until hard and completely cool, about 30 minutes.

4. Place chocolate chips and shortening in small microwave-safe bowl. Microwave at MEDIUM (50%) 45 seconds or until smooth when stirred. Spoon about 2 teaspoons into each cup; use pastry brush or spoon to coat inside. Refrigerate 20 minutes or until coating is set.

5. Meanwhile, combine pudding mix, milk and lemon extract in medium bowl. Beat with whisk or on low speed of mixer 2 minutes. Fold in thawed non-dairy whipped topping; refrigerate 30 minutes or until set. Spoon scant ½ cup lemon cream filling into each cup. Garnish with shredded lemon peel, if desired.

HERSHEY'S

Merry Chocolate Nut Clusters

Makes about 3 dozen candies

1 cup HERSHEY'S SPECIAL DARK Chocolate Chips or
   HERSHEY'S Semi-Sweet Chocolate Chips

½ cup HERSHEY'S Premier White Chips

1 tablespoon shortening (do not use butter, margarine,
   spread or oil)

2¼ cups (11½-oz. pkg.) lightly salted peanuts, divided

1. Place chocolate chips, white chips and shortening in small microwave-safe bowl. Microwave at MEDIUM (50%) 1 minute; stir. If necessary, microwave at MEDIUM an additional 15 seconds at a time, stirring after each heating, or until chips are melted and mixture is smooth when stirred. Reserve ¼ cup peanuts for garnish; stir remaining peanuts into chocolate mixture.

2. Drop by teaspoons into 1-inch candy papers; top each candy with a reserved peanut. Refrigerate, uncovered, until chocolate is set, about 1 hour. Store in airtight container in cool, dry place.

HERSHEY'S

Baked Apple Slices with Peanut Butter Crumble

Makes 6 to 8 servings

    4 cups peeled and thinly sliced apples
    1 cup sugar, divided
    1 cup all-purpose flour, divided
    3 tablespoons butter or margarine, divided
    1 cup quick-cooking or old-fashioned rolled oats
  ½ teaspoon ground cinnamon
    1 cup REESE'S Creamy Peanut Butter
       Sweetened whipped cream or ice cream (optional)

1. Heat oven to 350°F. Grease 9-inch square baking pan.

2. Stir together apples, ¾ cup sugar and ¼ cup flour in large bowl. Spread in prepared pan; dot with 2 tablespoons butter. Combine oats, remaining ¾ cup flour, remaining ¼ cup sugar and cinnamon in medium bowl; set aside.

3. Place remaining 1 tablespoon butter and peanut butter in small microwave-safe bowl. Microwave at MEDIUM (50%) 30 seconds or until butter is melted; stir until smooth. Add to oat mixture; blend until crumbs are formed. Sprinkle crumb mixture over apples.

4. Bake 40 to 45 minutes or until apples are tender and edges are bubbly. Cool slightly. Serve warm or cool with whipped cream or ice cream, if desired

HERSHEY'S

Chocolate & Peanut Butter Truffles

Makes about 3½ dozen candies

¾ cup (1½ sticks) butter (not shortening, margarine, oil or spreads)

1 cup REESE'S Peanut Butter Chips

½ cup HERSHEY'S Cocoa

1 can (14 oz.) sweetened condensed milk (not evaporated milk)

1 tablespoon vanilla extract

HERSHEY'S Cocoa or finely chopped nuts or graham cracker crumbs

1. Melt butter and peanut butter chips in large saucepan over very low heat, stirring often. Add cocoa; stir until smooth. Stir in sweetened condensed milk; stir constantly about 4 minutes or until mixture is thick and glossy. Remove from heat; stir in vanilla. Transfer mixture to medium bowl.

2. Refrigerate 2 hours or until firm enough to handle. Shape into 1-inch balls; roll in cocoa, nuts or graham cracker crumbs. Refrigerate until firm, about 1 hour. Store, covered, in refrigerator.

HERSHEY'S

Toffee-Banana Rum Bread

Makes 2 loaves

2½   cups all-purpose flour
1   cup sugar
3½   teaspoons baking powder
1   teaspoon salt
½   cup plus 2 tablespoons milk
¼   cup vegetable oil
2   tablespoons rum or 2 teaspoons rum extract
1   egg
1   cup mashed ripe banana (about 3 medium bananas)
1   cup chopped nuts
1⅓   cups (8-oz. pkg.) HEATH BITS 'O BRICKLE Toffee Bits, divided

1. Heat oven to 350°F. Grease and flour two 8½×4½×2½-inch loaf pans.

2. Stir together flour, sugar, baking powder and salt in large bowl. Add milk, oil, rum, egg and banana; stir with spoon until well blended. Stir in nuts. Spread 1¼ cups batter in bottom of each prepared pan. Top each batter with ½ cup toffee bits. Gently spread about 1 cup remaining batter into each pan. Sprinkle remaining bits over batter.

3. Bake 30 to 35 minutes or until wooden pick inserted into center comes out clean. (Bread will sink slightly in center.) Remove from oven to wire rack. With knife, loosen bread from sides of pan. Cool 10 minutes; remove from pans. Cool completely.

HERSHEY'S

Deep Dark Chocolate Soufflé

Makes 6 servings

- ½ cup plus 3 tablespoons sugar, divided
- ½ cup HERSHEY'S SPECIAL DARK Cocoa
- ¼ cup all-purpose flour
- 1 cup milk
- ¼ cup (½ stick) butter or margarine
- 1 teaspoon vanilla extract
- 4 eggs, separated
    Coffee ice cream*

*Or other favorite flavor ice cream

1. Heat oven to 350°F. Butter 6-cup soufflé dish; coat with 1 tablespoon sugar.

2. Stir together cocoa and flour in small bowl; set aside. Heat milk and butter in medium saucepan until butter melts and mixture is very hot (do not boil). Reduce heat; gradually add cocoa mixture, beating with whisk until well blended and thick. Remove from heat; stir in ½ cup sugar and vanilla. Cool slightly. Add egg yolks, one at a time, beating well after each addition. Cool to room temperature.

3. Beat egg whites in large bowl until foamy; gradually add remaining 2 tablespoons sugar and continue beating until stiff. Stir small amount beaten whites into chocolate mixture; fold chocolate mixture into remaining whites. Carefully pour into prepared dish.

4. Bake 40 to 45 minutes or until puffy. Serve immediately with ice cream.

HERSHEY'S

Classic Boston Cream Pie

Makes 8 to 10 servings

⅓ **cup shortening**
1 **cup sugar**
2 **eggs**
1 **teaspoon vanilla extract**
1¼ **cups all-purpose flour**
1½ **teaspoons baking powder**
¼ **teaspoon salt**
¾ **cup milk**
   Rich Filling (recipe follows)
   Dark Cocoa Glaze (recipe follows)

1. Heat oven to 350°F. Grease and flour one 9-inch round baking pan.

2. Beat shortening, sugar, eggs and vanilla in large bowl until fluffy. Stir together flour, baking powder and salt; add alternately with milk to shortening mixture. Pour batter into prepared pan.

3. Bake 30 to 35 minutes or until wooden pick inserted into center comes out clean. Cool 10 minutes; remove from pan to wire rack. Cool completely.

4. Prepare Rich Filling. Using long serrated knife, cut cake horizontally into two even layers. Place 1 layer on serving plate, cut side up; spread filling over layer. Top with remaining layer, cut side down. Prepare Dark Cocoa Glaze. Pour glaze over top of cake, allowing glaze to drizzle down sides. Refrigerate several hours or until cold. Cover; refrigerate leftover dessert.

(recipe continued on page 176)

Rich Filling

Makes about 2 cups filling

- ⅓ **cup sugar**
- 2 **tablespoons cornstarch**
- 1½ **cups milk**
- 2 **egg yolks, slightly beaten**
- 1 **tablespoon butter or margarine**
- 1 **teaspoon vanilla extract**

Stir together sugar and cornstarch in medium saucepan; gradually add milk and egg yolks, stirring until blended. Cook over medium heat, stirring constantly, until mixture comes to a boil. Boil and stir 1 minute. Remove from heat; stir in butter and vanilla. Cover; refrigerate several hours until cold.

Dark Cocoa Glaze

Makes about ¾ cup glaze

- 3 **tablespoons water**
- 2 **tablespoons butter or margarine**
- 3 **tablespoons HERSHEY'S Cocoa**
- 1 **cup powdered sugar**
- ½ **teaspoon vanilla extract**

Heat water and butter in small saucepan over medium heat until mixture begins to boil; remove from heat. Stir in cocoa immediately. Gradually add powdered sugar and vanilla, beating with whisk until smooth; cool slightly.

HERSHEY'S

Chocolate Cream Squares

Makes 9 to 12 servings

1¼ cups graham cracker crumbs
⅓ cup plus ¼ cup HERSHEY'S Cocoa, divided
⅔ cup plus ¼ cup sugar, divided
⅓ cup butter or margarine, melted
1 package (3 oz.) cream cheese, softened
1 teaspoon vanilla extract
⅓ cup milk
1 tub (8 oz.) frozen non-dairy whipped topping, thawed

1. Stir together graham cracker crumbs, ¼ cup cocoa, ¼ cup sugar and ⅓ cup melted butter in medium bowl. Reserve ¼ cup crumbs. Press remaining crumbs onto bottom of 9-inch square pan.

2. Beat cream cheese, remaining ⅔ cup sugar and vanilla in medium bowl until well blended. Add remaining ⅓ cup cocoa alternately with milk, beating until smooth. Gradually fold in whipped topping until well combined. Spoon over prepared crust. Sprinkle reserved crumbs over top.

3. Cover; refrigerate 6 to 8 hours or until set. Cut into squares.

HERSHEY'S

Chocolate Toffee Crunch Squares

Makes 3 dozen squares

4 cups (2 11.5-oz. pkgs.) HERSHEY'S Milk Chocolate Chips
1 cup HEATH BITS 'O BRICKLE Toffee Bits
1 cup salted peanuts
1 cup halved pretzel sticks
½ cup MOUNDS Sweetened Coconut Flakes (optional)
½ cup HERSHEY'S Premier White Chips
1 teaspoon shortening (not butter, margarine, spread or oil)
Paper candy cups (optional)

1. Line 9-inch square pan with plastic wrap. Place chocolate chips in large microwave-safe bowl. Microwave at MEDIUM (50%) 1 minute; stir. If necessary, microwave at MEDIUM an additional 15 seconds at a time, stirring after each heating, just until chips are melted and mixture is smooth when stirred. Immediately add toffee bits, peanuts, pretzels and coconut, if desired; stir to coat.

2. Spread mixture into prepared pan; cover with plastic wrap or foil. Refrigerate 45 minutes or until firm.

3. Place white chips and shortening in small microwave-safe bowl. Microwave at MEDIUM 30 seconds; stir. If necessary, microwave at MEDIUM an additional 10 seconds at a time, stirring after each heating, just until chips are melted and mixture is smooth when stirred. Using fork, drizzle white chips mixture over chocolate mixture in pan. Cover; refrigerate 5 minutes or until firm.

4. Bring to room temperature. Remove chocolate mixture from pan and place right-side up on cutting board; remove plastic

HERSHEY'S

wrap. Cut into 1¹/₂-inch squares. Place each square in a candy cup, if desired. Store in covered container in a cool place.

VARIATION: CHOCOLATE TOFFEE HAYSTACKS: Prepare chocolate mixture as above. Instead of spreading into square pan, drop chocolate mixture by slightly heaping tablespoons onto wax paper-lined cookie sheet or tray. Refrigerate until firm. Melt white chips as directed above; drizzle over haystacks.

HERSHEY'S

Dark Fudgey Pecan Pie

Makes 8 servings

    1 unbaked 9-inch pie crust
 1½ cups coarsely chopped pecans
   ½ cup (1 stick) butter or margarine
    1 cup light corn syrup
    1 cup sugar
   ½ cup HERSHEY'S SPECIAL DARK Cocoa
    4 eggs
    1 teaspoon vanilla extract

1. Heat oven to 325°F. Fit pie crust into 9-inch pie plate according to package directions; fold edges under and crimp. Spread pecans evenly on bottom of pastry shell.

2. Combine butter, corn syrup, sugar and cocoa in medium saucepan; cook over low heat, stirring constantly, until sugar dissolves. Cool slightly. Stir in eggs and vanilla until blended. Pour into crust.

3. Bake 1 hour and 10 minutes or until set. Cool. Serve with whipped cream, if desired.

NOTE: To prevent overbrowning, cover edge of pie with foil.

HERSHEY'S

Timeless Treasures

CONTENTS

HERSHEY'S

CAKES AND CHEESECAKES

Petit Mocha Cheesecakes

CRUMB CRUST (recipe follows)

1 package (8 oz.) cream cheese, softened

1 cup sugar

2 eggs

1 teaspoon vanilla extract

⅓ cup HERSHEY'S Cocoa

2 tablespoons all-purpose flour

1 tablespoon powdered instant coffee

1 teaspoon hot water

CHOCOLATE GLAZE (recipe follows, optional)

1. Heat oven to 375°F. Line small muffin cups (1¾ inches in diameter) with paper baking cups.

2. Prepare CRUMB CRUST. Place 1 slightly heaping teaspoon crumb mixture into each cup; press lightly. Beat cream cheese in large bowl until fluffy. Add sugar, eggs and vanilla; beat well. Add cocoa and flour; beat well. Dissolve coffee in water; add to chocolate mixture. Place about 1 tablespoon chocolate mixture into each cup.

3. Bake 15 to 18 minutes or until just set. Cool completely in pan on wire rack. Drizzle with CHOCOLATE GLAZE, if desired. Refrigerate until cold, about 2 hours. Cover; refrigerate leftover cheesecakes.

CRUMB CRUST: Stir together ½ cup graham cracker crumbs, 2 tablespoons powdered sugar and 2 tablespoons melted butter or margarine in small bowl until well combined.

CHOCOLATE GLAZE: Combine ¼ cup HERSHEY'S SPECIAL DARK Chocolate Chips or HERSHEY'S Semi-Sweet Chocolate Chips and 2 tablespoons whipping cream in small saucepan. Cook over very low heat, stirring constantly, until smooth. Use immediately.

Makes 42 cheesecakes

Chocolate Almond Cheesecake

ALMOND CRUMB
  CRUST (recipe
  follows)
3 packages (8 oz. each)
  cream cheese,
  softened
1¼ cups sugar
½ cup dairy sour cream
⅓ cup HERSHEY'S Cocoa
2 tablespoons all-
  purpose flour
3 eggs
2 teaspoons almond
  extract
1 teaspoon vanilla
  extract
ALMOND WHIPPED
  CREAM (recipe
  follows)
Sliced almonds
  (optional)

1. Prepare ALMOND CRUMB CRUST.

2. Increase oven temperature to 425°F. Combine cream cheese, sugar, sour cream, cocoa and flour in large bowl; beat on medium speed of mixer until smooth. Add eggs, almond extract and vanilla; beat well. Pour into prepared crust.

3. Bake 10 minutes. Reduce oven temperature to 250°F; continue baking 55 minutes or until center appears set. Remove from oven to wire rack. With knife, loosen cake from side of pan. Cool completely; remove side of pan.

4. Refrigerate several hours before serving. Garnish with ALMOND WHIPPED CREAM and sliced almonds, if desired. Cover; refrigerate leftover cheesecake.

ALMOND CRUMB CRUST: Heat oven to 350°F. Stir together ¾ cup vanilla wafer crumbs (about 20 wafers), ½ cup ground blanched almonds and 3 tablespoons sugar in small bowl; stir in 3 tablespoons melted butter or margarine. Press mixture firmly onto bottom and ½ inch up side of 9-inch springform pan. Bake 8 to 10 minutes; cool slightly.

ALMOND WHIPPED CREAM: Combine ½ cup cold whipping cream, 2 tablespoons powdered sugar, ¼ teaspoon vanilla extract and ⅛ teaspoon almond extract in small bowl; beat until stiff. Makes 1 cup whipped cream.

Makes 10 to 12 servings

Peanut Butter Holiday Cheesecake

6 tablespoons butter or margarine, melted

6 tablespoons HERSHEY'S Cocoa

⅓ cup powdered sugar

1½ cups (about 45 cookies) vanilla wafer cookie crumbs

1 package (8 oz.) cream cheese, softened

2 tablespoons lemon juice

1½ cups REESE'S Peanut Butter Chips

1 can (14 oz.) sweetened condensed milk (not evaporated milk)

1 cup (½ pt.) whipping cream, whipped

CRANBERRY TOPPING (recipe follows)

1. Stir together butter, cocoa, powdered sugar and vanilla wafer crumbs in bowl. Press firmly onto bottom of 9-inch springform pan; refrigerate while preparing filling.

2. Beat cream cheese and lemon juice in large bowl until fluffy; set aside. Combine peanut butter chips and sweetened condensed milk in medium saucepan over low heat; stir constantly until chips are melted and mixture is smooth. Add to cream cheese mixture; blend well. Fold in whipped cream. Pour evenly over crumb crust.

3. Cover; refrigerate while preparing CRANBERRY TOPPING. Spread topping evenly over cheesecake. Cover; refrigerate several hours or overnight. Remove side of springform pan to serve. Cover; refrigerate leftover cheesecake.

Makes 12 to 14 servings

Cranberry Topping

2 cups fresh or frozen cranberries

1 cup sugar

¾ cup water, divided

2 tablespoons cornstarch

1 teaspoon vanilla extract

1. Stir together cranberries, sugar and ½ cup water in medium saucepan. Cook over medium heat, stirring occasionally, until mixture comes to a boil. Reduce heat; simmer 3 minutes. Remove from heat.

2. Stir together cornstarch and remaining ¼ cup water; gradually add to cranberry mixture. Return to heat; stir constantly until mixture thickens and resembles fruit preserves (about 4 minutes). Cool to room temperature; stir in vanilla.

Makes about 3½ cups topping

Black Forest
Mini Cheesecakes

18 to 24 vanilla wafer
  cookies
2 packages (8 oz. each)
  cream cheese,
  softened
1¼ cups sugar
⅓ cup HERSHEY'S Cocoa
2 tablespoons all-
  purpose flour
3 eggs
1 container (8 oz.) dairy
  sour cream
½ teaspoon almond
  extract
  SOUR CREAM
  TOPPING (recipe
  follows)
  Canned cherry pie
  filling, chilled

1. Heat oven to 325°F. Line muffin cups (2½ inches in diameter) with foil baking cups. Place 1 vanilla wafer (flat-side down) in bottom of each cup.

2. Beat cream cheese in large bowl until smooth. Add sugar, cocoa and flour; blend well. Add eggs; beat well. Stir in sour cream and almond extract. Fill each muffin cup almost full with batter.

3. Bake 20 to 25 minutes or until set. Remove from oven; cool 5 to 10 minutes. Spread heaping teaspoon SOUR CREAM TOPPING on each cup. Cool completely in pan on wire rack; refrigerate. Just before serving, garnish with cherry pie filling. Cover; refrigerate leftover cheesecakes.

SOUR CREAM TOPPING: Stir together 1 container (8 oz.) dairy sour cream, 2 tablespoons sugar and 1 teaspoon vanilla extract in small bowl until sugar is dissolved.

Makes 18 to 24 cheesecakes

Molten Chocolate-Cherry Cakes

CHOCOLATE DIPPED
CHERRIES (recipe
follows)
⅔ cup plus 1 tablespoon
sugar, divided
¾ cup (1½ sticks) butter
or margarine
½ cup HERSHEY'S Cocoa
¼ cup whipping cream
1½ teaspoons vanilla
extract
¼ cup all-purpose flour
2 eggs
2 egg yolks
⅓ cup maraschino
cherries, finely
chopped
Sweetened whipped
cream (optional)

1. Prepare CHOCOLATE DIPPED CHERRIES.

2. Heat oven to 400°F. Grease six ¾-cup soufflé dishes or six 6-ounce custard cups. Sprinkle inside of each with some of the 1 tablespoon sugar. Place dishes in a 13×9-inch baking pan or a jelly-roll pan.

3. Melt butter in medium saucepan. Remove from heat. Whisk in cocoa, ⅓ cup sugar, whipping cream and vanilla. Whisk in flour just until combined. Set aside.

4. Beat eggs, egg yolks and remaining ⅓ cup sugar in large bowl on high speed of mixer about 5 minutes or until slightly thickened and lemon-colored. Beat in chocolate mixture on medium speed. Pour about ¼ cup into each prepared dish. Sprinkle chopped cherries evenly over each. Carefully pour remaining chocolate mixture into each dish.

5. Bake 13 to 15 minutes or just until top of each cake looks dry. (Do not overbake.) Let stand in dishes 3 minutes. Loosen sides of each. Invert onto serving plates. Serve warm topped with whipped cream and a CHOCOLATE DIPPED CHERRY.

CHOCOLATE DIPPED CHERRIES: Drain 6 maraschino cherries with stems. Pat dry with paper towels. Place ¼ cup HERSHEY'S SPECIAL DARK Chocolate Chips or HERSHEY'S Semi-Sweet Chocolate Chips and ½ teaspoon shortening (do not use butter, margarine, spread or oil) in small microwave-safe bowl. Microwave

at MEDIUM (50%) for 45 seconds. Stir until chips are melted. Dip cherries into chocolate mixture. Place on wax paper-lined tray. Refrigerate until serving time.

Tip: For make-ahead convenience, prepare the cakes but do not bake. Cover with plastic wrap and refrigerate for up to 3 hours. Let stand at room temperature 30 minutes, then bake as directed.

Makes 6 servings

Orange-Glazed Cocoa Bundt Cake

¾ cup (1½ sticks) butter or margarine, softened
1⅔ cups sugar
2 eggs
1 teaspoon vanilla extract
¾ cup dairy sour cream
2 cups all-purpose flour
⅔ cup HERSHEY'S Cocoa
½ teaspoon salt
2 teaspoons baking soda
1 cup buttermilk or sour milk*
ORANGE GLAZE (recipe follows)

1. Heat oven to 350°F. Grease and flour 12-cup fluted tube pan.

2. Beat butter, sugar, eggs and vanilla in large bowl until light and fluffy; stir in sour cream. Stir together flour, cocoa and salt. Stir baking soda into buttermilk in medium bowl; add alternately with dry ingredients to butter mixture. Beat 2 minutes on medium speed. Pour batter into prepared pan.

3. Bake 50 minutes or until wooden pick inserted into center comes out clean. Cool in pan 10 minutes. Remove from pan to wire rack. Cool completely. Glaze with ORANGE GLAZE; garnish as desired.

ORANGE GLAZE: Combine 2 cups powdered sugar, ¼ cup melted butter or margarine, 3 tablespoons orange juice, 1 teaspoon vanilla extract and ½ teaspoon freshly grated orange peel in medium bowl; beat until smooth. Makes 1 cup glaze.

VARIATION: VANILLA GLAZE: Substitute 3 tablespoons water for orange juice and omit orange peel.

*To sour milk: Use 1 tablespoon white vinegar plus milk to equal 1 cup.

Makes 12 to 14 servings

Easy Chocolate Layer Cake

2 packages (4 oz. each) HERSHEY'S SPECIAL DARK Chocolate Premium Baking Bar, broken into pieces
3 cups all-purpose flour
1½ cups sugar
2 teaspoons baking soda
1 teaspoon salt
2 cups water
⅔ cup vegetable oil
2 tablespoons white vinegar
2 teaspoons vanilla extract

1. Heat oven to 350°F. Grease and flour two 9-inch round baking pans; line bottoms with waxed paper.

2. Place chocolate in small microwave-safe bowl. Microwave at MEDIUM (50%) 1½ to 2 minutes or until chocolate is melted when stirred; cool slightly.

3. Stir together flour, sugar, baking soda and salt in large bowl. Add melted chocolate, water, oil, vinegar and vanilla; beat on medium speed of mixer until well blended. Pour into prepared pans.

4. Bake 30 to 35 minutes or until wooden pick inserted in center comes out clean. Cool 10 minutes; remove from pans to wire racks. Cool completely. Frost as desired.

Makes 10 to 12 servings

Whipped Chocolate Frosting

2 packages (4 oz. each)
    HERSHEY'S
    SPECIAL DARK
    Chocolate Premium
    Baking Bar, broken
    into pieces
½ cup whipping cream
½ cup (1 stick) butter,
    softened
2 cups powdered sugar
1 teaspoon vanilla
    extract

1. Place chocolate and whipping cream in medium microwave-safe bowl. Microwave at MEDIUM (50%) 1½ to 2 minutes, until chocolate is melted and mixture is smooth when stirred; refrigerate until thoroughly chilled.

2. Beat butter in large bowl; gradually beat in powdered sugar and vanilla until thoroughly blended and creamy. Gradually add chocolate mixture, beating until stiff; use immediately. Cover; keep refrigerated.

Makes about 3½ cups frosting

Rich HEATH Bits Cheesecake

VANILLA WAFER
CRUST (recipe
follows)
3 packages (8 oz. each)
cream cheese,
softened
1 cup sugar
3 eggs
1 container (8 oz.) dairy
sour cream
½ teaspoon vanilla
extract
1⅓ cups (8-oz. pkg.)
HEATH Milk
Chocolate Toffee Bits,
divided

1. Prepare VANILLA WAFER CRUST. Heat oven to 350°F.

2. Beat cream cheese and sugar in large bowl on medium speed of mixer until well blended. Add eggs, 1 at a time, beating well after each addition. Add sour cream and vanilla; beat on low speed until blended.

3. Pour half of cheese mixture into crust. Reserve ¼ cup toffee bits for topping; sprinkle remaining toffee bits over cheese mixture in pan. Spoon in remaining cheese mixture.

4. Bake 1 hour or until filling is set. Cool 15 minutes. Sprinkle reserved toffee bits over top. With knife, loosen cake from side of pan. Cool completely; remove side of pan. Cover; refrigerate at least 4 hours before serving. Cover; refrigerate leftover cheesecake.

VANILLA WAFER CRUST: Combine 1¾ cups vanilla wafer crumbs (about 55 wafers) and 2 tablespoons sugar; stir in ¼ cup (½ stick) melted butter or margarine. Press onto bottom and 1 inch up side of 9-inch springform pan. Refrigerate about 30 minutes.

Makes 12 to 16 servings

Spicy Butterscotch Snack Cake

1 cup (2 sticks) butter or margarine, softened

1 cup sugar

2 eggs

½ teaspoon vanilla extract

½ cup applesauce

2½ cups all-purpose flour

1½ to 2 teaspoons ground cinnamon

1 teaspoon baking soda

½ teaspoon salt

1¾ cups (11-oz. pkg.) HERSHEY'S Butterscotch Chips

1 cup chopped pecans (optional)

Powdered sugar or frozen whipped topping, thawed (optional)

1. Heat oven to 350°F. Lightly grease 13×9×2-inch baking pan.

2. Beat butter and sugar in large bowl on medium speed of mixer until well blended. Add eggs and vanilla; beat well. Mix in applesauce. Stir together flour, cinnamon, baking soda and salt; gradually add to butter mixture, beating until well blended. Stir in butterscotch chips and pecans, if desired. Spread in prepared pan.

3. Bake 35 to 40 minutes or until wooden pick inserted in center comes out clean. Cool completely in pan on wire rack. Sprinkle with powdered sugar or serve with whipped topping, if desired.

Makes 12 to 16 servings

HERSHEY'S "PERFECTLY CHOCOLATE" Chocolate Cake

2 cups sugar

1¾ cups all-purpose flour

¾ cup HERSHEY'S Cocoa

1½ teaspoons baking powder

1½ teaspoons baking soda

1 teaspoon salt

2 eggs

1 cup milk

½ cup vegetable oil

2 teaspoons vanilla extract

1 cup boiling water

"PERFECTLY CHOCOLATE" CHOCOLATE FROSTING (recipe on page 199)

1. Heat oven to 350°F. Grease and flour two 9-inch round baking pans.

2. Stir together sugar, flour, cocoa, baking powder, baking soda and salt in large bowl. Add eggs, milk, oil and vanilla; beat on medium speed of mixer 2 minutes. Stir in boiling water (batter will be thin). Pour batter into prepared pans.

3. Bake 30 to 35 minutes or until wooden pick inserted in center comes out clean. Cool 10 minutes; remove from pans to wire racks. Cool completely. Frost with "PERFECTLY CHOCOLATE" CHOCOLATE FROSTING.

VARIATIONS:

ONE-PAN CAKE: Grease and flour 13×9×2-inch baking pan. Heat oven to 350°F. Pour batter into prepared pan. Bake 35 to 40 minutes. Cool completely. Frost.

THREE LAYER CAKE: Grease and flour three 8-inch round baking pans. Heat oven to 350°F. Pour batter into prepared pans. Bake 30 to 35 minutes. Cool 10 minutes; remove from pans to wire racks. Cool completely. Frost.

BUNDT CAKE: Grease and flour 12-cup fluted tube pan. Heat oven to 350°F. Pour batter into prepared pan. Bake 50 to 55 minutes. Cool 15 minutes; remove from pan to wire rack. Cool completely. Frost.

CUPCAKES: Line muffin cups (2½ inches in diameter) with paper baking cups. Heat oven to 350°F. Fill cups two-thirds full with batter. Bake 22 to 25 minutes. Cool completely. Frost. Makes 30 cupcakes.

Makes 10 to 12 servings

Apple-Chip Snacking Cake

2 eggs
½ cup vegetable oil
¼ cup apple juice
1 teaspoon vanilla
   extract
1¾ cups all-purpose flour
1 cup granulated sugar
½ teaspoon baking soda
½ teaspoon ground
   cinnamon
½ teaspoon salt
1½ cups chopped, peeled
   tart apples
¾ cup HERSHEY'S
   SPECIAL DARK
   Chocolate Chips,
   HERSHEY'S Semi-
   Sweet Chocolate
   Chips or HERSHEY'S
   Mini Chips Semi-
   Sweet Chocolate
½ cup chopped nuts
   Powdered sugar or
   whipped topping and
   ground cinnamon
   (optional)

1. Heat oven to 350°F. Grease and flour 8- or 9-inch square baking pan.

2. Beat eggs slightly in large bowl; add oil, apple juice and vanilla. Stir together flour, granulated sugar, baking soda, cinnamon and salt; stir into batter until blended. Add apples, chocolate chips and nuts; stir until well blended. Pour batter into prepared pan.

3. Bake 40 to 45 minutes or until cake begins to pull away from sides of pan. Cool completely in pan on wire rack. Sprinkle with powdered sugar or top with whipped topping sprinkled with cinnamon, if desired.

Makes 9 servings

"PERFECTLY CHOCOLATE" Chocolate Frosting

½ cup (1 stick) butter or
   margarine
⅔ cup HERSHEY'S Cocoa
3 cups powdered sugar
⅓ cup milk
1 teaspoon vanilla
   extract

Melt butter. Stir in cocoa. Alternately add powdered sugar and milk, beating to spreading consistency. Add small amount additional milk, if needed. Stir in vanilla.

Makes 2 cups frosting

5-Way Chocolate Cake

½ cup (1 stick) butter or margarine, softened

½ cup shortening

2¼ cups sugar

2 eggs

1 teaspoon vanilla extract

2½ cups all-purpose flour

⅔ cup HERSHEY'S Cocoa

1½ teaspoons baking soda

½ teaspoon baking powder

1 teaspoon salt

2 cups buttermilk or sour milk*

1. Choose one of the 5 ways for baking cake. Heat oven to 350°F. For cake, generously grease and flour baking pan(s). For cupcakes, do not grease or flour; line muffin cups (2½ inches in diameter) with paper baking cups.

2. Beat butter, shortening and sugar in large bowl until fluffy. Add eggs and vanilla; beat well. Stir together flour, cocoa, baking soda, baking powder and salt. Add to butter mixture alternately with buttermilk, beginning and ending with dry ingredients, beating until well blended.

3. Pour batter into prepared pan(s). For cupcakes, fill muffin cups half full with batter. Bake as follows:

Three 8-inch layer pans	30 to 35 minutes
One 13×9×2-inch pan	55 to 65 minutes
One 10-inch tube pan	55 to 65 minutes
Two 9×5×3-inch loaf pans	50 to 60 minutes
3½ dozen cupcakes	18 to 22 minutes

Cool cakes 10 minutes; remove from pan(s) to wire racks. Cupcakes can be removed immediately from pans to wire racks. Cool completely. Frost as desired.

To sour milk: Use 2 tablespoons white vinegar plus milk to equal 2 cups

Three Layer Cheesecake Squares

CHOCOLATE CRUMB CRUST (recipe follows)

3 packages (8 oz. each) cream cheese, softened

¾ cup sugar

3 eggs

⅓ cup dairy sour cream

3 tablespoons all-purpose flour

1 teaspoon vanilla extract

1 cup REESE'S Peanut Butter Chips, melted

1 cup HERSHEY'S SPECIAL DARK Chocolate Chips or HERSHEY'S Semi-Sweet Chocolate Chips, melted

1 cup HERSHEY'S Premier White Chips, melted

THREE LAYER DRIZZLE (recipe follows)

1. Heat oven to 350°F. Line 9-inch square baking pan with foil, extending edges over pan sides; grease lightly. Prepare CHOCOLATE CRUMB CRUST. Bake 8 minutes; cool slightly.

2. Beat cream cheese and sugar until smooth. Gradually add eggs, sour cream, flour and vanilla; beat well. Stir 1⅓ cups batter into melted peanut butter chips; pour into prepared crust. Stir 1⅓ cups batter into melted chocolate chips; carefully spoon over peanut butter layer. Stir remaining batter into melted white chips; carefully spoon over chocolate layer.

3. Bake 40 to 45 minutes or until almost set. Cool completely on wire rack.

4. Prepare THREE LAYER DRIZZLE. Drizzle, 1 flavor at a time, over cheesecake. Refrigerate about 3 hours or until drizzle is firm. Use foil to lift cheesecake out of pan; cut into squares. Cover; refrigerate leftover cheesecake.

CHOCOLATE CRUMB CRUST: Combine 1½ cups (about 45 wafers) vanilla wafer crumbs, 6 tablespoons powdered sugar, 6 tablespoons HERSHEY'S Cocoa and 6 tablespoons melted butter or margarine. Press onto bottom of pan.

THREE LAYER DRIZZLE: Melt 1 tablespoon REESE'S Peanut Butter Chips with ½ teaspoon shortening, stirring until chips are melted and mixture is smooth. Repeat with 1 tablespoon HERSHEY'S SPECIAL DARK Chocolate Chips or HERSHEY'S Semi-Sweet Chocolate Chips with ½ teaspoon shortening and 1 tablespoon HERSHEY'S Premier White Chips with ½ teaspoon shortening.

Makes 9 to 12 servings

COOKIES

Peanut Butter Fun Filled Cookies

½ cup (1 stick) butter or margarine, softened

¾ cup sugar

⅓ cup REESE'S Creamy Peanut Butter

1 egg

½ teaspoon vanilla extract

1¼ cups all-purpose flour

½ teaspoon baking soda

¼ teaspoon salt

1⅓ cups (8-oz. pkg.) REESE'S Milk Chocolate Baking Pieces Filled with Peanut Butter Crème

1. Heat oven to 350°F.

2. Beat butter, sugar and peanut butter in large bowl until creamy. Add egg and vanilla; beat well. Stir together flour, baking soda and salt; add to butter mixture, blending well. Stir in baking pieces. Drop by heaping teaspoons onto ungreased cookie sheet.

3. Bake 12 to 14 minutes or until light golden brown around the edges. Cool 1 minute; remove from cookie sheet to wire rack. Cool completely.

Makes 36 cookies

Magnificent
Mini Bar Cookies

6 tablespoons butter, softened

⅓ cup butter flavored shortening

½ cup packed light brown sugar

⅓ cup granulated sugar

1 egg

1½ teaspoons vanilla extract

1½ cups all-purpose flour

½ teaspoon baking soda

½ teaspoon salt

1⅓ cups (8-oz. pkg.) HERSHEY'S Mini Milk Chocolate Bars,* divided

¾ cup chopped nuts (optional)

5 to 6 HERSHEY'S Milk Chocolate Bars (1.55 oz. each) may be substituted for the mini milk chocolate bars. Cut bars into about ½-inch pieces and proceed as above.

1. Heat oven to 350°F.

2. Beat butter and shortening in large bowl until well blended. Add brown sugar and granulated sugar; beat thoroughly. Add egg and vanilla, beating until well blended. Stir together flour, baking soda and salt; gradually beat into butter mixture. Stir in 1 cup mini chocolate bars** and nuts, if desired. Drop by rounded teaspoons onto ungreased cookie sheet.

3. Bake 10 to 12 minutes or until lightly browned. Cool slightly; remove from cookie sheet to wire rack. Cool additional 1 to 2 minutes; press 1 to 2 of the remaining chocolate bars onto the surface of each cookie. Cool completely.

**The entire bag of small chocolate bars can be stirred in; omit topping baked cookies with additional chocolate bars.

Makes 36 cookies

Almond Shortbread Cookies with Chocolate Filling

¾ cup sliced almonds, toasted*

1 cup (2 sticks) butter or margarine, softened

¾ cup sugar

3 egg yolks

¾ teaspoon almond extract

2 cups all-purpose flour
CHOCOLATE FILLING (recipe follows)
Powdered sugar (optional)

*To toast almonds: Heat oven to 350°F. Spread almonds in thin layer in shallow baking pan. Bake 8 to 10 minutes, stirring occasionally, until light golden brown; cool.

**HERSHEY'S Semi-Sweet Chocolate Chips or HERSHEY'S SPECIAL DARK Chocolate Chips may also be used.

1. Finely chop almonds; set aside.

2. Beat butter and sugar in large bowl until creamy. Add egg yolks and almond extract; beat well. Gradually add flour, beating until well blended. Stir in almonds. Refrigerate dough 1 to 2 hours or until firm enough to handle.

3. Heat oven to 350°F. On well-floured surface, roll about one-fourth of dough to about ⅛-inch thickness (keep remaining dough in refrigerator). Using 2-inch round cookie cutter, cut into equal number of rounds. Place on ungreased cookie sheet.

4. Bake 8 to 10 minutes or until almost set. Cool slightly; remove from cookie sheet to wire rack. Cool completely. Spread about 1 teaspoon CHOCOLATE FILLING onto bottom of 1 cookie. Top with second cookie; gently press together. Repeat with remaining cookies. Allow filling to set, about 1 hour. Lightly sift powdered sugar over top of cookies, if desired. Cover; store at room temperature.

Makes 44 sandwich cookies

CHOCOLATE FILLING: Combine 1 cup HERSHEY'S Milk Chocolate Chips** and ⅓ cup whipping cream in small saucepan. Stir constantly over low heat until mixture is smooth. Remove from heat. Cool about 20 minutes or until slightly thickened and spreadable. About 1 cup filling.

Chocolate Dipped Toffee Bits Cookies

2¼ cups all-purpose flour

1 teaspoon baking soda

½ teaspoon salt

½ cup (1 stick) butter or margarine, softened

¾ cup granulated sugar

¾ cup packed light brown sugar

1 teaspoon vanilla extract

2 eggs

1⅓ cups (8-oz. pkg.) HEATH BITS 'O BRICKLE Toffee Bits

1¾ cups (10-oz. pkg.) HERSHEY'S Mini KISSES BRAND Milk Chocolates

2 tablespoons shortening (do not use butter, margarine, spread or oil)

1. Heat oven to 350°F. Lightly grease cookie sheet.

2. Stir together flour, baking soda and salt; set aside. Beat butter, granulated sugar, brown sugar and vanilla in large bowl until well blended. Add eggs; beat well. Gradually add flour mixture, beating until well blended. Stir in toffee bits. Drop by rounded teaspoons onto prepared cookie sheet.

3. Bake 9 to 11 minutes or until lightly browned. Cool slightly; remove from cookie sheet to wire rack. Cool completely.

4. Line tray with wax paper. Place chocolates and shortening in medium, microwave-safe bowl. Microwave at MEDIUM (50%) 1 minute; stir. If necessary, microwave at MEDIUM an additional 15 seconds at a time, stirring after each heating, until chocolates are melted and mixture is smooth when stirred.

5. Dip about one-third of each cookie into melted chocolate. Shake gently and scrape cookie bottom on edge of bowl to remove excess chocolate. Place on prepared tray. Refrigerate until chocolate is firm, about 30 minutes. Store in cool, dry place with wax paper between layers of cookies.

Makes 48 cookies

Classic
Mini KISSES Cookies
(Cookie Mix in a Jar)

2¼ cups all-purpose flour

¾ cup granulated sugar

1 teaspoon baking soda

½ teaspoon salt

1½ cups HERSHEY'S Mini KISSES BRAND Milk Chocolates, divided

¾ cup packed light brown sugar

BAKING INSTRUCTIONS (recipe follows)

To increase shelf life of mix, wrap brown sugar in plastic wrap and press into place.

Use clean 1-quart (4-cup) glass jar with lid. Stir together flour, granulated sugar, baking soda and salt; pack down into bottom of jar. Layer with 1 cup HERSHEY'S MINI KISSES BRAND Milk Chocolates and then brown sugar.* Top with remaining ½ cup chocolates; close jar. Attach card with following instructions:

BAKING INSTRUCTIONS:

1. Heat oven to 375°F. Spoon contents of jar into large bowl; break up any lumps with spoon, stirring until mixture is crumbly.

2. Add 1 cup (2 sticks) softened butter, cut into pieces, and 1 teaspoon vanilla extract; stir with wooden spoon until crumbly mixture forms. Add 2 lightly beaten eggs; stir until smooth, very stiff dough forms. Drop by heaping teaspoons onto ungreased cookie sheet.

3. Bake 8 to 10 minutes or until lightly browned. Cool slightly; remove from cookie sheet to wire rack. Cool completely.

Makes 36 cookies

Chocolate Thumbprint Cookies

½ cup (1 stick) butter or margarine, softened

⅔ cup sugar

1 egg, separated

2 tablespoons milk

1 teaspoon vanilla extract

1 cup all-purpose flour

⅓ cup HERSHEY'S Cocoa

¼ teaspoon salt

1 cup chopped nuts

VANILLA FILLING (recipe follows)

26 HERSHEY'S KISSES BRAND Milk Chocolates or HERSHEY'S HUGS BRAND Chocolates

1. Beat butter, sugar, egg yolk, milk and vanilla in medium bowl until fluffy. Stir together flour, cocoa and salt; gradually add to butter mixture, beating until blended. Refrigerate dough at least 1 hour or until firm enough to handle.

2. Heat oven to 350°F. Lightly grease cookie sheet. Shape dough into 1-inch balls. With fork, beat egg white slightly. Dip each ball into egg white; roll in nuts. Place on prepared cookie sheet. Press thumb gently in center of each cookie.

3. Bake 10 to 12 minutes or until set. Meanwhile, prepare VANILLA FILLING. Remove wrappers from chocolate pieces. Remove cookies from cookie sheet to wire rack; cool 5 minutes. Spoon about ¼ teaspoon filling into each thumbprint. Gently press chocolate piece in center of each cookie. Cool completely.

Makes 24 cookies

VANILLA FILLING: Combine ½ cup powdered sugar, 1 tablespoon softened butter or margarine, 2 teaspoons milk and ¼ teaspoon vanilla extract in small bowl; beat until smooth.

VARIATION: Omit egg white and chopped nuts. Roll balls in granulated sugar. Bake as directed. Top with VANILLA FILLING and pecan or walnut half.

Chocolate-Cherry
Slice 'n' Bake Cookies

¾ cup (1½ sticks) butter
  or margarine, softened
1 cup sugar
1 egg
1½ teaspoons vanilla
  extract
2¼ cups all-purpose flour
2 teaspoons baking
  powder
½ teaspoon salt
¼ cup finely chopped
  maraschino cherries
½ teaspoon almond
  extract
  Red food color
⅓ cup HERSHEY'S Cocoa
¼ teaspoon baking soda
4 teaspoons water
  COCOA ALMOND GLAZE
  (recipe on page 212)

1. Beat butter, sugar, egg and vanilla in large bowl until fluffy. Stir together flour, baking powder and salt; gradually add to butter mixture, beating until mixture forms a smooth dough. Remove 1¼ cups dough to medium bowl; blend in cherries, almond extract and about 6 drops food color.

2. Stir together cocoa and baking soda. Add with water to remaining dough; blend until smooth. Divide chocolate dough in half; roll each half between 2 sheets of wax paper, forming 12×4½-inch rectangle. Remove top sheet of wax paper from each rectangle. Divide cherry mixture in half; with floured hands, shape each half into 12-inch roll. Place 1 roll in center of each rectangle; wrap chocolate dough around each roll. Wrap each roll in plastic wrap. Refrigerate about 6 hours.

3. Heat oven to 350°F. Cut rolls into ¼-inch-thick slices; place on ungreased cookie sheet.

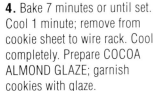

4. Bake 7 minutes or until set. Cool 1 minute; remove from cookie sheet to wire rack. Cool completely. Prepare COCOA ALMOND GLAZE; garnish cookies with glaze.

Makes 90 cookies

Really Minty Brownie Drops

⅔ cup shortening

1⅓ cups packed light brown sugar

1 tablespoon water

1 teaspoon vanilla extract

2 eggs

1¼ cups all-purpose flour

⅓ cup HERSHEY'S SPECIAL DARK Cocoa or HERSHEY'S Cocoa

½ teaspoon salt

¼ teaspoon baking soda

1⅓ cups (8-oz. pkg.) YORK Mini Peppermint Patties*

1. Heat oven to 350°F.

2. Beat shortening, brown sugar, water and vanilla in large bowl on medium speed of mixer until well blended. Add eggs; beat well.

3. Stir together flour, cocoa, salt and baking soda. Gradually add to sugar mixture, beating on low speed just until blended. Stir in peppermint patties. Drop by rounded tablespoons 2 inches apart onto ungreased cookie sheet.

4. Bake 7 to 9 minutes or until cookies are set. Cookies will appear soft and moist. Do not overbake. Cool 2 minutes; remove from cookie sheet to wire rack. Cool completely.

Makes 42 cookies

16 to 17 small (½ inch) YORK Peppermint Patties, unwrapped and coarsely chopped, may be substituted for the mini peppermint patties. Line cookie sheets with parchment paper. Follow above baking directions, but slide baked cookies and parchment paper onto wire rack to cool completely. Peel cookies from paper.

Cocoa Almond Glaze

2 tablespoons butter or margarine

2 tablespoons HERSHEY'S Cocoa

2 tablespoons water

1 cup powdered sugar

⅛ teaspoon almond extract

1. Melt butter in small saucepan over low heat. Add cocoa and water; stir constantly until mixture thickens. Do not boil.

2. Remove from heat; gradually add powdered sugar and almond extract, beating with whisk until smooth and of desired consistency. Add additional water, ½ teaspoon at a time, if needed.

About ½ cup glaze

Grandma's Favorite Sugarcakes

⅔ cup butter or margarine, softened

1½ cups packed light brown sugar

1 cup granulated sugar

2 eggs

2 teaspoons vanilla extract

4½ cups all-purpose flour

2 teaspoons baking soda

1 teaspoon baking powder

1 teaspoon salt

1 cup buttermilk or sour milk*

2 cups (12-oz. pkg.) HERSHEY'S Mini Chips Semi-Sweet Chocolate

2 cups chopped walnuts or pecans

Vanilla frosting (optional)

Colored sugar or sprinkles (optional)

1. Heat oven to 350°F. Grease cookie sheet.

2. Beat butter, brown sugar and sugar until well blended in large mixing bowl. Add eggs and vanilla; beat until creamy. Stir together flour, baking soda, baking powder and salt; add alternately with buttermilk to butter mixture, beating well after each addition. Stir in small chocolate chips and nuts. Drop by level ¼ cupfuls or heaping tablespoons 2 inches apart onto prepared cookie sheet.

3. Bake 12 to 14 minutes or until golden brown. Frost with favorite vanilla frosting; garnish with colored sugar, if desired.

*To sour milk: Use 1 tablespoon white vinegar plus milk to equal 1 cup.

Makes 36 cookies

Nutty Blossoms

1 cup (2 sticks) butter or margarine, softened

½ cup granulated sugar

1 teaspoon vanilla extract

1¾ cups all-purpose flour

1 cup finely chopped almonds or walnuts

Powdered sugar

48 HERSHEY'S KISSES BRAND Milk Chocolates, unwrapped

1. Heat oven to 350°F. Beat butter, granulated sugar and vanilla in large bowl until fluffy. Add flour and almonds; beat on low speed of mixer until well blended.

2. Shape dough into 1-inch balls. Roll in powdered sugar; place on ungreased cookie sheet.

3. Bake 13 to 15 minutes or until cookies are set but not browned. Immediately press a chocolate into center of each cookie; cookie will crack around edges. Remove from cookie sheet to wire rack. Cool completely.

Makes 48 cookies

Iceberg Cookies

1 family-size (13×9-inch pan) original supreme brownie mix with HERSHEY'S Syrup
¼ cup HERSHEY'S Cocoa
2 eggs
1 tablespoon vegetable oil
1 tablespoon water
Powdered sugar
1⅓ cups (8-oz. pkg.) HERSHEY'S Dark Chocolate Baking Pieces Filled with Raspberry Crème or REESE'S Milk Chocolate Baking Pieces Filled with Peanut Butter Crème*

*HERSHEY'S Mini KISSES BRAND Milk Chocolates, HERSHEY'S Mini Milk Chocolate Bars or any of HERSHEY'S baking pieces may also be used. Press one Mini KISS, mini milk chocolate bar or several baking chips into center of cookie. Allow to soften 3 to 5 minutes; press additional pieces into softened baking pieces.

1. Lightly grease cookie sheets or line with parchment paper.

2. Beat brownie mix, pouch of syrup, cocoa, eggs, oil and water in medium bowl until well blended. Cover; refrigerate about 1 hour or until thoroughly chilled (dough will still be sticky).

3. Heat oven to 350°F. Shape dough into 1-inch balls. (Return dough to refrigerator if necessary or drop by rounded teaspoons onto wax paper-lined trays and refrigerate about 10 minutes.) Roll balls in powdered sugar; place on prepared cookie sheet.

4. Bake 9 to 11 minutes or until set. Cool slightly; press 1 baking piece into center of each cookie. Remove from cookie sheet to wire rack. Allow baking piece to soften several minutes; stir with wooden pick to blend center filling and chocolate. Gently place 2 to 3 baking pieces into melted center. Cool completely.

Makes 48 cookies

PIES AND DESSERTS

Creamy Milk Chocolate Pudding Pie

1⅓ cups (8-oz. pkg.)
   HERSHEY'S Mini
   Milk Chocolate Bars,*
   divided

⅔ cup sugar

6 tablespoons cornstarch

2 tablespoons
   HERSHEY'S Cocoa

½ teaspoon salt

4 egg yolks

3 cups milk

2 tablespoons butter or
   margarine, softened

1 tablespoon vanilla
   extract

1 packaged chocolate
   crumb crust (6 oz.)
   Sweetened whipped
   cream or whipped
   topping

6 HERSHEY'S Milk Chocolate Bars (1.55 oz. each) may be substituted for the mini milk chocolate bars. Set aside 6 to 8 chocolate bar sections to use as garnish; proceed as above.

1. Set aside ¼ cup small chocolate bars for garnish. Stir together sugar, cornstarch, cocoa and salt in 2-quart saucepan. Combine egg yolks and milk in bowl or container with pouring spout. Gradually blend milk mixture into sugar mixture.

2. Cook over medium heat, stirring constantly, until mixture comes to a boil. Boil and stir 1 minute. Remove from heat; stir in butter and vanilla. Add remaining chocolate bars; stir until bars are melted and mixture is well blended. Pour into crumb crust; press plastic wrap onto filling. Cool. Refrigerate several hours or until chilled and firm. Remove plastic wrap and garnish with whipped cream and reserved small chocolate bars. Cover; refrigerate leftovers.

Makes 6 to 8 servings

Easy Chip and Nut Gift Bread

2 cups all-purpose flour
1 cup sugar
1 teaspoon baking powder
1 teaspoon salt
½ teaspoon baking soda
1 cup applesauce
½ cup shortening
2 eggs
1 cup HERSHEY'S Cinnamon Chips, HERSHEY'S SPECIAL DARK Chocolate Chips or HERSHEY'S Semi-Sweet Chocolate Chips
½ cup chopped walnuts
   Powdered sugar (optional)

1. Heat oven to 350°F. Grease three 5¾×3¼×2-inch mini loaf pans.

2. Combine flour, sugar, baking powder, salt, baking soda, applesauce, shortening and eggs in large bowl. Beat on medium speed of mixer until well blended. Stir in cinnamon chips and walnuts. Divide batter evenly into prepared pans.

3. Bake 45 minutes or until wooden pick inserted in center comes out clean. Cool 10 minutes; remove from pans to wire rack. Cool completely. Sift with powdered sugar, if desired.

Makes 3 small loaves

Candy Cups

1⅓ cups (8-oz. pkg.) HERSHEY'S Premier White Chips and Macadamia Nuts

1. Place chip and nut mixture in medium microwave-safe bowl. Microwave at MEDIUM (50%) 30 seconds; stir. If necessary, microwave at MEDIUM an additional 15 seconds at a time, stirring after each heating, until chips are melted and mixture is blended when stirred.

2. Drop by rounded teaspoons into small paper candy cups. (Mixture may also be dropped onto wax paper-lined cookie sheet.) Cool until set. Store in cool, dry place.

VARIATION: *½ cup chopped sweetened dried cranberries or dried apricots (or combination of the two) may be stirred into melted chip mixture. Proceed as above.*

Makes 12 candies

Double Peanut Clusters

1⅔ cups (10-oz. pkg.)
   REESE'S Peanut
   Butter Chips
1 tablespoon shortening
   (do not use butter,
   margarine, spread
   or oil)
2 cups salted peanuts

1. Line cookie sheet with waxed paper.

2. Place peanut butter chips and shortening in large microwave-safe bowl. Microwave at MEDIUM (50%) 1½ minutes; stir until chips are melted and mixture is smooth. If necessary, microwave an additional 30 seconds until chips are melted when stirred. Stir in peanuts.

3. Drop by rounded teaspoons onto prepared cookie sheet. (Mixture may also be dropped into small candy paper cups.) Cool until set. Store in a cool, dry place.

VARIATION: *Butterscotch Nut Clusters: Follow above directions, substituting 1⅔ cups (10-oz. pkg.) HERSHEY'S Butterscotch Chips.*

Makes about 2½ dozen snacks

Macadamia Nut Fudge

1½ cups sugar

1 jar (7 oz.) marshmallow crème

1 can (5 oz.) evaporated milk (about ⅔ cup)

¼ cup (½ stick) butter or margarine

2 bags (8 oz. each) HERSHEY'S SPECIAL DARK Chips and Macadamia Nuts

½ teaspoon vanilla extract

1. Line 8- or 9-inch square pan with foil, extending foil over edges of pan.

2. Combine sugar, marshmallow crème, evaporated milk and butter in heavy medium saucepan. Cook over medium heat, stirring constantly, to a full boil. Boil, stirring constantly, 5 minutes.

3. Remove from heat; add macadamia nut mix and vanilla. Stir just until chips are melted; pour into prepared pan.

4. Refrigerate 1 hour or until firm. Lift fudge out of pan using foil; place on cutting board. Cut into squares. Store tightly covered in a cool, dry place.

Makes 2 pounds fudge

Chocolate Marbled Peanut Butter Pie

- ½ cup REESE'S Creamy Peanut Butter
- 1 package (3 oz.) cream cheese, softened
- ½ teaspoon vanilla extract
- 1 cup powdered sugar
- ½ cup milk
- 1 tub (8 oz.) frozen non-dairy whipped topping, thawed
- ½ cup HERSHEY'S SPECIAL DARK Chocolate Chips or HERSHEY'S Semi-Sweet Chocolate Chips
- 1 extra serving-size packaged graham crumb crust (9 oz.)

1. Beat peanut butter, cream cheese and vanilla in medium bowl on medium speed of mixer until smooth. Gradually add powdered sugar and milk, beating until smooth. Fold in whipped topping. Place 1 cup peanut butter mixture in separate bowl. Spread remaining mixture in crust.

2. Place chocolate chips in small microwave-safe bowl. Microwave at MEDIUM (50%) 30 seconds or until chocolate is melted and smooth when stirred. Stir chocolate into reserved peanut butter mixture, blending thoroughly; drop by tablespoons onto top of pie. Using knife or spatula, gently swirl for marbled effect.

3. Cover; freeze 4 to 5 hours or until firm. Garnish as desired.

Makes 6 to 8 servings

Chocolate Quicky Sticky Bread

2 loaves (16 oz. each) frozen bread dough

¾ cup granulated sugar

1 tablespoon HERSHEY'S Cocoa

1 teaspoon ground cinnamon

½ cup (1 stick) butter or margarine, melted and divided

½ cup packed light brown sugar

¼ cup water

HERSHEY'S Mini KISSES BRAND Milk Chocolates

1. Thaw loaves as directed on package; let rise until doubled.

2. Stir together granulated sugar, cocoa and cinnamon. Stir together ¼ cup butter, brown sugar and water in small microwave-safe bowl. Microwave at HIGH (100%) 30 to 60 seconds or until smooth when stirred. Pour mixture into 12-cup fluted tube pan.

3. Heat oven to 350°F. Pinch off pieces of bread dough; form into balls, 1½ inches in diameter, placing 3 chocolates inside each ball. Dip each ball in remaining ¼ cup butter; roll in cocoa-sugar mixture. Place balls in prepared pan.

4. Bake 45 to 50 minutes or until golden brown. Cool 20 minutes in pan; invert onto serving plate. Cool until lukewarm.

Makes 12 servings

Chocolate Peanut Butter Fudge Topping

1 cup HERSHEY'S Milk Chocolate Chips

1 cup REESE'S Peanut Butter Chips

½ cup whipping cream

2 tablespoons light corn syrup

1 teaspoon vanilla extract

1. Stir together milk chocolate chips, peanut butter chips, whipping cream and corn syrup in medium microwave-safe bowl. Microwave at HIGH (100%) 1 to 1½ minutes or until chips are melted and mixture is smooth when stirred. If necessary, microwave an additional 30 seconds at a time, stirring after each heating, just until mixture is smooth when stirred. Stir in vanilla. Serve warm over ice cream.

Makes 1⅔ cups sauce

Mocha Brownie Nut Torte

1 cup (2 sticks) butter

1 package (4 oz.) HERSHEY'S Unsweetened Chocolate Premium Baking Bar, broken into pieces

4 eggs

1 teaspoon vanilla extract

2 cups granulated sugar

1 cup all-purpose flour

1 cup finely chopped pecans

1 package (8 oz.) cream cheese, softened

1 cup powdered sugar

½ cup chilled whipping cream

2 to 3 teaspoons powdered instant coffee

CHOCOLATE GLAZE (recipe follows)

1. Heat oven to 350°F. Line bottom and sides of 9-inch round cake pan with foil, extending foil beyond sides. Grease foil.

2. Place butter and unsweetened baking chocolate in medium microwave-safe bowl. Microwave at MEDIUM (50%) 1 minute; stir. If necessary, microwave an additional 15 seconds at a time, stirring after each heating, until chocolate is melted when stirred. Cool 5 minutes.

3. Beat eggs and vanilla in large bowl until foamy. Gradually beat in granulated sugar. Blend in chocolate mixture; fold in flour and pecans. Spread mixture in prepared pan. Bake 40 to 45 minutes or until wooden pick inserted in center comes out clean. Cool completely in pan on wire rack.

4. Use foil to lift brownie from pan; remove foil. Place brownie layer on serving plate. Beat cream cheese and powdered sugar in medium bowl until well blended. Beat whipping cream and instant coffee until stiff; gradually fold into cream cheese mixture, blending well. Spread over brownie layer. Cover; refrigerate until serving time.

5. Just before serving, prepare CHOCOLATE GLAZE. Drizzle generous tablespoon glaze over top and down sides of each serving.

Makes 10 to 12 servings

CHOCOLATE GLAZE: Place 6 oz. (1½ 4-oz. bars) HERSHEY'S SPECIAL DARK Chocolate Premium Baking Bar and ½ cup whipping cream in small microwave-safe bowl. Microwave at MEDIUM 30 to 45 seconds or until chocolate is melted and mixture is smooth when stirred. Cool slightly.

Makes 1 cup glaze

Chocolate Harvest Nut Pie

½ cup packed light brown sugar

⅓ cup HERSHEY'S Cocoa

¼ teaspoon salt

1 cup light corn syrup

3 eggs

3 tablespoons butter or margarine, melted

1½ teaspoons vanilla extract

½ cup coarsely chopped pecans

½ cup coarsely chopped walnuts

¼ cup slivered almonds

1 unbaked 9-inch pie crust

Whipped topping (optional)

1. Heat oven to 350°F. Stir together brown sugar, cocoa and salt. Add corn syrup, eggs, butter and vanilla; stir until well blended. Stir in pecans, walnuts and almonds. Pour into unbaked pie crust. To prevent overbrowning of crust, cover edge of pie with foil.

2. Bake 30 minutes. Remove foil. Bake additional 25 to 30 minutes or until puffed across top. Remove from oven to wire rack. Cool completely.

3. Garnish with whipped topping and additional nuts, if desired. Cover; store leftover pie in refrigerator.

Makes 8 servings

Fudge Bottomed Chocolate Layer Pie

1 cup HERSHEY'S SPECIAL DARK Chocolate Chips, divided

6 tablespoons milk, divided

1 packaged chocolate crumb crust (6 oz.)

1½ cups miniature marshmallows

1 tub (8 oz.) frozen non-dairy whipped topping, thawed and divided

Additional sweetened whipped cream or whipped topping (optional)

1. Place ⅓ cup chocolate chips and 2 tablespoons milk in microwave-safe bowl. Microwave 30 seconds at MEDIUM (50%); stir. If necessary, microwave an additional 15 seconds at a time, stirring after each heating, until chips are melted and mixture is smooth when stirred. Spread on bottom of crust. Refrigerate while preparing next step.

2. Place marshmallows, remaining ⅔ cup chocolate chips and remaining 4 tablespoons milk in small saucepan. Cook over medium heat, stirring constantly, until marshmallows are melted and mixture is well blended. Transfer to separate large bowl; cool completely.

3. Stir 2 cups whipped topping into cooled chocolate mixture; spread 2 cups mixture over chocolate in crust. Blend remaining whipped topping and remaining chocolate mixture; spread over surface of pie.

4. Cover; freeze several hours or until firm. Garnish as desired. Cover; freeze remaining pie.

Makes 6 to 8 servings

Fudge Walnut Brownie Pie

2 eggs

1 cup sugar

½ cup (1 stick) butter, melted

1 teaspoon vanilla extract

⅔ cup all-purpose flour

⅓ cup HERSHEY'S Cocoa

¼ teaspoon salt

1 cup HERSHEY'S SPECIAL DARK Chocolate Chips or HERSHEY'S Semi-Sweet Chocolate Chips

½ cup chopped walnuts
Ice cream
HERSHEY'S Syrup

1. Heat oven to 350°F. Lightly grease 9-inch pie plate.

2. Beat eggs in large bowl; stir in sugar, butter and vanilla. Stir together flour, cocoa and salt; stir into butter mixture. Stir in chocolate chips and walnuts. Pour into prepared pie plate.

3. Bake 30 to 35 minutes or until set. Cool. Serve warm or at room temperature with ice cream; drizzle syrup over top.

Note: In place of pie plate, batter can be baked in lightly greased 8-inch square baking pan. Bake at 350°F for 30 to 35 minutes or until brownies begin to pull away from sides of pan.

Makes 6 to 8 servings

Layers of Mint
Chocolate Grasshopper Pie

1⅓ cups (8-oz. pkg.) YORK Mini Peppermint Patties,* divided

5 tablespoons milk, divided

1 packaged chocolate crumb crust (6 oz.)

1½ cups miniature marshmallows

1 tub (8 oz.) frozen non-dairy whipped topping, thawed and divided

Additional sweetened whipped cream or whipped topping (optional)

16 to 17 small (1½ inch) YORK Peppermint Patties, unwrapped, may be substituted for the mini peppermint patties. Set aside 1 to 2 patties for garnish; coarsely chop remaining patties and proceed as above.

1. Place ⅓ cup peppermint patties and 1 tablespoon milk in microwave-safe bowl. Microwave 30 seconds at MEDIUM (50%); stir. If necessary, microwave an additional 15 seconds at a time, stirring after each heating, until chips are melted and mixture is smooth when stirred. Spread on bottom of crust. Refrigerate while preparing next step.

2. Place marshmallows, ⅔ cup peppermint patties and remaining 4 tablespoons milk in small saucepan. Cook over medium heat, stirring constantly, until marshmallows are melted and mixture is well blended. Transfer to separate large bowl; cool completely.

3. Stir 2 cups whipped topping into cooled chocolate mixture; spread over chocolate in crust. Set aside about 2 tablespoons peppermint patties; coarsely chop the remaining patties. Stir chopped pieces into remaining whipped topping. Spread over surface of pie.

4. Cover; freeze several hours or until firm. Garnish with remaining peppermint patties and additional whipped topping, if desired. Cover; freeze remaining pie.

Makes 6 to 8 servings

Chicken Satay Skewers

6 garlic cloves, chopped

4 teaspoons dried coriander

4 teaspoons light brown sugar

2 teaspoons salt

1½ teaspoons HERSHEY'S Cocoa

1 teaspoon ground black pepper

½ cup soy sauce

6 tablespoons vegetable oil

2 tablespoons lime juice

4 teaspoons fresh, chopped ginger

2½ pounds boneless, skinless chicken breasts

PEANUT DIPPING SAUCE (recipe on page 238)

¼ cup fresh cilantro, chopped (optional)

1. Combine garlic, coriander, brown sugar, salt, cocoa and pepper in large bowl. Stir in soy sauce, oil, lime juice and ginger.

2. Cut chicken into 1½- to 2-inch cubes. Add to soy sauce mixture, stirring to coat chicken pieces. Cover; marinate in refrigerator for at least 2 hours.

3. Meanwhile, prepare PEANUT DIPPING SAUCE. Thread chicken pieces onto satay sticks. Grill or broil, basting with marinade. Discard leftover marinade. Garnish with chopped cilantro, if desired. Serve with prepared peanut sauce. Refrigerate leftovers.

**Makes 15 to 20 appetizers or
4 to 6 entrée servings**

Sloppy Dawg Sauce

3 tablespoons butter or margarine

1 cup finely chopped onion

¾ cup ketchup

¼ cup packed light brown sugar

3 tablespoons HERSHEY'S Cocoa

3 tablespoons Worchestershire sauce

1 tablespoon tomato paste

1 tablespoon white vinegar

¼ teaspoon dry mustard

¼ teaspoon hot pepper sauce

1. Melt butter in heavy medium saucepan over medium heat; add onion. Cook until tender. Stir in ketchup, brown sugar, cocoa, Worchestershire sauce, tomato paste, vinegar, mustard and hot pepper sauce.

2. Heat to boiling, stirring occasionally; remove from heat. Serve warm as a topping for grilled hot dogs, burgers, chicken or steak. If sauce starts to become too thick, add water 1 tablespoon at a time. Refrigerate leftovers.

Makes 2 cups sauce

Peanut Dipping Sauce

1 cup REESE'S Creamy Peanut Butter

½ cup peanut oil

¼ cup lime juice

¼ cup soy sauce

3 tablespoons honey

2 garlic cloves, minced

1 teaspoon cayenne pepper

½ teaspoon hot pepper sauce

Gradually whisk peanut oil into peanut butter in medium bowl. Blend in lime juice, soy sauce, honey, garlic, cayenne pepper and hot pepper sauce. Adjust flavors to taste. (You should have a sweet/hot flavor.)

Makes 2¼ cups dipping sauce

HERSHEY'S Secret Ingredient Chili

¼ cup vegetable oil

1½ cups chopped onion

2 pounds lean ground beef or ground turkey

2 tablespoons HERSHEY'S Cocoa

2 tablespoons chili powder

2 teaspoons ground cayenne pepper

1 teaspoon salt

½ teaspoon ground allspice

½ teaspoon ground cinnamon

2 cans (28 oz. each) whole tomatoes, undrained

1 can (12 oz.) tomato paste

1 cup water

2 cans (about 15 oz. each) red kidney beans, drained (optional)

Additional chopped onion (optional)

Shredded Cheddar cheese (optional)

1. In 5-quart saucepan, over medium heat, heat oil; add onion. Cook, stirring frequently, 3 minutes or until tender. Add meat; cook until brown. Drain.

2. Stir in cocoa, seasonings, tomatoes with liquid, tomato paste and water; heat to boiling. Reduce heat; simmer 30 minutes.

3. Serve plain, topped with beans, sprinkled with additional chopped onion, topped with cheese or all of the above.

Makes 12 servings

Smokey Chili with Pasta

Smokey Chili with Pasta

2 cups (about 6 oz.) rotelle or rotini pasta, uncooked

1 pound ground beef

1 cup chopped onion

2 cans (10¾ oz. each) condensed tomato soup

2 cans (about 15 oz. each) red kidney beans

2 tablespoons HERSHEY'S Cocoa

2¼ teaspoons chili powder

¾ teaspoon ground black pepper

½ teaspoon salt

Grated Parmesan cheese (optional)

1. Cook pasta according to package directions; drain.

2. Meanwhile, cook ground beef and onion until meat is thoroughly done and onion is tender. If necessary, drain fat.

3. Stir in soup, undrained kidney beans, cocoa, chili powder, pepper and salt. Heat to boiling; reduce heat. Stir in hot pasta; heat thoroughly. Serve with Parmesan cheese, if desired.

Makes 8 servings

Spiced Cocoa Seasoning

3 tablespoons HEATH BITS 'O BRICKLE Toffee Bits

8 tablespoons paprika

6 tablespoons onion powder

5 tablespoons black pepper

3 tablespoons HERSHEY'S Cocoa

3 tablespoons salt

2½ tablespoons dried oregano

2½ tablespoons dried thyme

½ teaspoon cayenne pepper

1. Place toffee bits in food processor or blender. Cover; process until toffee bits are very fine.

2. Combine toffee, paprika, onion powder, black pepper, cocoa, salt, oregano, thyme and cayenne pepper in medium bowl.

3. Store in airtight container in cool dry place for up to 6 weeks. Apply as a dry rub or seasoning for poultry, pork, beef, seafood, salads, soups or vegetables.

Makes 1⅔ cups seasoning

Ranch Style Shrimp and Bacon Appetizers

RANCH STYLE
BARBECUE SAUCE
(recipe follows)
30 large peeled, deveined
shrimp
½ pound thick-cut bacon
10 wooden skewers*

*To prevent wooden skewers from burning while grilling or broiling, soak in water about 10 minutes before using.

1. Prepare RANCH STYLE BARBECUE SAUCE.

2. Wrap each shrimp with ½ bacon strip. Thread 3 wrapped shrimp onto each wooden skewer.

3. Grill or broil shrimp skewers until bacon is cooked and shrimp is no longer translucent, but has turned pink. Baste with barbecue sauce. Return to heat to warm sauce. Serve with additional barbecue sauce, if desired.

Makes 10 shrimp skewers

Ranch Style Barbecue Sauce

¼ cup vegetable or olive oil
½ cup minced onion
2 garlic cloves, minced
2 tablespoons lemon juice
1 tablespoon ground black
pepper
1 teaspoon dry mustard
1 teaspoon paprika
½ teaspoon hot pepper sauce
½ teaspoon salt
1½ cups ketchup
1 cup HEATH BITS 'O
BRICKLE Toffee Bits
¼ cup cider vinegar
3 tablespoons sugar
1½ tablespoons HERSHEY'S
Cocoa

1. Heat oil in large saucepan over medium heat; add onion and garlic. Cook until tender. Stir in lemon juice, black pepper, mustard, paprika, hot pepper sauce and salt. Simmer for 5 minutes; reduce heat.

2. Stir in ketchup, toffee bits, vinegar, sugar and cocoa. Simmer 15 minutes. Refrigerate leftovers.

Makes 3 cups sauce

Cocoa-Coffee Spiced Chicken with Salsa Mole

2 tablespoons ground coffee beans

2 tablespoons HERSHEY'S Cocoa

1 tablespoon salt

1 teaspoon chili powder

1 tablespoon brown sugar

1 tablespoon vegetable oil

4 boneless, skinless chicken breasts

SALSA MOLE (recipe follows)

Cilantro sprigs (optional)

Black beans (optional)

Rice (optional)

1. Heat oven to 425°F. Grease baking sheet.

2. Stir together coffee beans, cocoa, salt, chili powder and brown sugar. Rub chicken pieces with vegetable oil; pat on cocoa mixture. Place coated chicken pieces on prepared baking sheet.

3. Bake 20 to 25 minutes or until juices are clear. Meanwhile, prepare SALSA MOLE.

4. Arrange chicken and salsa on large platter. Garnish with cilantro sprigs, if desired. Serve with black beans and rice, if desired.

Makes 4 servings

Salsa Mole

2 tomatoes, chopped

1 avocado, peeled and diced

1 green onion, minced

1 tablespoon snipped cilantro

1 clove garlic, pressed

¼ cup HERSHEY'S Mini Chips Semi-Sweet Chocolate

1 teaspoon lime juice

Stir together tomatoes, avocado, onion, cilantro, garlic, small chocolate chips and lime juice in medium bowl.

Spicy Cocoa Glazed Pecans

¼ cup plus 2 tablespoons sugar, divided
1 cup water
1½ cups pecan halves or pieces
1 tablespoon HERSHEY'S Cocoa
3 to 4 teaspoons chili powder
⅛ to ¼ teaspoon cayenne pepper

1. Heat oven to 350°F. Lightly spray shallow baking pan with vegetable oil spray.

2. Stir together ¼ cup sugar and warm water, stirring until sugar dissolves. Add pecans; let soak 10 minutes. Drain water and discard.

3. Stir together remaining 2 tablespoons sugar, cocoa, chili powder and cayenne pepper in medium bowl. Add pecans; toss until all the cocoa mixture coats the pecans. Spread coated pecans on prepared pan.

4. Bake 10 to 15 minutes or until pecans start to glisten and appear dry. Stir occasionally while baking. Cool completely. Store in cool, dry place. Serve as a snack with beverages or sprinkle in salads.

Makes 1½ cups coated pecans

Spicy Cocoa Sloppy Joes

1½ pounds lean ground beef

1 to 1¼ cups chopped onion

1 cup ketchup

2 tablespoons HERSHEY'S Cocoa

1½ tablespoons yellow mustard

2½ teaspoons chili powder

1½ teaspoons ground black pepper

1¼ teaspoons salt

1. Cook ground beef and onion in large skillet over medium heat until beef is browned and onion is tender. Drain excess fat.

2. Stir in ketchup, cocoa, mustard, chili powder, pepper and salt. Heat 10 to 15 minutes on low heat or until hot. Serve in buns. Cover; refrigerate leftovers.

Makes 4½ cups sandwich filling

Tex-Mex Spiced Cocoa Vegetable Rub

2 tablespoons TEX-MEX SPICED RUB (recipe follows)

1 yellow pepper, cored and seeded

1 red pepper, cored and seeded

1 large red onion

1 mango, firm but not hard, peeled

1 yellow squash

1 zucchini

15 grape tomatoes

1 large portobello mushroom, sliced lengthwise

¾ cup vinaigrette dressing, purchased or prepared

1. Heat oven to 450°F.

2. Cut yellow pepper, red pepper, onion, mango, yellow squash and zucchini into 1-inch pieces. Place in large bowl. Add tomatoes and mushroom.

3. Pour vinaigrette dressing and spice mix over vegetables; toss.

4. Spread vegetables in shallow baking pan. Bake 20 to 30 minutes or until vegetables are fork tender.

Makes 6 servings

Tex-Mex Spiced Rub

½ cup HEATH BITS 'O BRICKLE Toffee Bits

½ cup chili powder

¼ cup paprika

1 tablespoon ground cumin

1 teaspoon garlic powder

1 teaspoon red pepper flakes

2 teaspoons salt

2 teaspoons dried oregano leaves

½ cup HERSHEY'S Cocoa

1 tablespoon ground coffee beans

1. Place toffee bits in food processor or blender. Cover; process until toffee bits are very fine.

2. Combine toffee and remaining ingredients in medium bowl; blend well. Place in airtight container.*

*Store in cool dry place for up to 4 months.

Makes 2 cups spice blend

Cocoa Spiced Beef Stir-Fry

2 cups beef broth

3 tablespoons soy sauce

2 tablespoons cornstarch

2 tablespoons HERSHEY'S Cocoa

2 teaspoons minced garlic (about 4 cloves)

1½ teaspoons ground ginger

1 teaspoon crushed red pepper flakes

1 pound boneless top round or flank beef steak

3 tablespoons vegetable oil, divided

1½ cups large onion pieces

1 cup carrot slices

3 cups fresh broccoli florets and pieces

1½ cups sweet red pepper slices

Hot cooked rice

Additional soy sauce

Cashew or peanut pieces (optional)

1. Stir together beef broth, soy sauce, cornstarch, cocoa, garlic, ginger and red pepper flakes; set aside. Cut beef steak into ¼-inch-wide strips.

2. Heat large skillet or wok over high heat about 1 minute or until hot. Drizzle about 1 tablespoon oil into pan; heat about 30 seconds. Add beef strips; stir-fry until well browned. Remove from heat; set aside.

3. Drizzle remaining 2 tablespoons oil into pan; add onion pieces and carrots. Stir-fry until onion is crisp but tender. Add broccoli and red pepper strips; cook until crisp-tender.

4. Return beef to pan; add broth mixture. Cook and stir until mixture comes to a boil and thickens. Serve over hot rice with additional soy sauce and cashew pieces, if desired.

Makes 4 to 6 servings

HERSHEY'S

Perfectly Peppermint Brownies

¾ cup HERSHEY'S Cocoa

½ teaspoon baking soda

⅔ cup butter or margarine, melted and divided

½ cup boiling water

2 cups sugar

2 eggs

1⅓ cups all-purpose flour

1 teaspoon vanilla extract

¼ teaspoon salt

1⅓ cups (8-oz. pkg.) YORK Mini Peppermint Patties*

16 to 17 small (1½ inch) YORK Peppermint Patties, unwrapped and coarsely chopped, may be substituted for the mini peppermint patties.

1. Heat oven to 350°F. Grease 13×9×2-inch baking pan.

2. Stir together cocoa and baking soda in large bowl; stir in ⅓ cup butter. Add boiling water; stir until mixture thickens. Stir in sugar, eggs and remaining ⅓ cup butter; stir until smooth. Add flour, vanilla and salt; blend completely. Stir in peppermint patties. Spread in prepared pan.

3. Bake 35 to 40 minutes or until brownies begin to pull away from sides of pan. Cool completely in pan on wire rack. Cut into bars.

Makes 36 brownies

Fudgey Almond Bars

¾ cup (1½ sticks) butter or margarine, softened

¾ cup powdered sugar

1½ cups all-purpose flour

⅓ cup butter or margarine

½ cup HERSHEY'S Cocoa

1 can (14 oz.) sweetened condensed milk (not evaporated milk)

1¼ cups almonds, toasted and coarsely chopped*

½ cup hot water

2 eggs, well beaten

¼ to ½ teaspoon almond extract

⅛ teaspoon salt

1. Heat oven to 350°F.

2. Beat ¾ cup butter and powdered sugar in large bowl until well blended. Add flour; mix well. Press mixture evenly onto bottom of ungreased 13×9×2-inch baking pan. Bake 15 to 18 minutes or until lightly browned.

3. Meanwhile, in medium saucepan over low heat, melt ⅓ cup butter. Add cocoa, stirring until smooth. Remove from heat; stir in sweetened condensed milk, almonds, water, eggs, almond extract and salt. Pour evenly over prepared crust. Return to oven.

4. Bake 25 to 30 minutes or until center is set. Cool completely in pan on wire rack. Cut into bars. Cover; store in refrigerator.

To toast almonds: Heat oven to 350°F. Spread almonds in thin layer in shallow baking pan. Bake 8 to 10 minutes, stirring occasionally, until light golden brown; cool.

Makes 24 to 36 bars

Layered Apricot Snacking Bars

2 cups (12-oz. pkg.) HERSHEY'S Premier White Chips, divided

1 package (6 oz.) dried apricots, cut into ¼-inch pieces

1 cup boiling water

½ cup (1 stick) margarine, softened

⅓ cup granulated sugar

¼ cup packed light brown sugar

1 egg

1 teaspoon vanilla extract

1 cup plus 2 tablespoons all-purpose flour, divided

¼ teaspoon baking soda

¼ teaspoon salt

½ cup wheat germ

2 tablespoons honey

1 egg white

½ teaspoon shortening

1. Heat oven to 350°F. Set aside ⅓ cup white chips for glaze.

2. Stir together apricots and water in small bowl; cover. Let stand 5 minutes; drain. Meanwhile, in large bowl, beat margarine, granulated sugar, brown sugar, egg and vanilla until well blended. Stir together 1 cup flour, baking soda and salt; gradually add to margarine mixture, beating until well blended. Stir in remaining 1⅔ cups white chips; press mixture onto bottom of ungreased 8-inch square baking pan. Spread softened apricots over cookie base. Stir together wheat germ, remaining 2 tablespoons flour, honey and egg white until blended; crumble over apricots.

3. Bake 30 minutes or until wheat germ is lightly browned. Cool completely in pan on wire rack.

4. Stir together reserved ⅓ cup white chips and shortening in small microwave-safe bowl. Microwave at MEDIUM (50%) 30 seconds; stir. If necessary, microwave at MEDIUM an additional 15 seconds at a time, stirring after each heating, just until chips are melted when stirred. Using tines of fork, drizzle mixture over top; let stand until glaze is firm. Cut into bars.

Makes 16 bars

Peanut Butter Chips and Jelly Bars

1½ cups all-purpose flour

½ cup sugar

¾ teaspoon baking powder

½ cup (1 stick) cold butter or margarine

1 egg, beaten

¾ cup grape jelly

1⅔ cups (10-oz. pkg.) REESE'S Peanut Butter Chips, divided

1. Heat oven to 375°F. Grease 9-inch square baking pan.

2. Stir together flour, sugar and baking powder; cut in butter with pastry blender or fork until mixture resembles coarse crumbs. Stir in beaten egg until blended.

3. Reserve 1 cup mixture; press remaining mixture onto bottom of prepared pan. Stir jelly to soften; spread evenly over crust. Sprinkle 1 cup peanut butter chips over jelly. Stir remaining ⅔ cup chips into reserved crumb mixture; sprinkle over top.

4. Bake 25 to 30 minutes or until lightly browned. Cool completely in pan on wire rack. Cut into bars.

HIGH ALTITUDE DIRECTIONS:
Increase flour to 1½ cups plus 1 tablespoon. Add 1 tablespoon water with egg. Do not change baking time or temperature.

Makes 16 bars

Chocolate Seven Layer Bars

1½ cups finely crushed thin pretzels or pretzel sticks

¾ cup (1½ sticks) butter or margarine, melted

1 can (14 oz.) sweetened condensed milk (not evaporated milk)

1 package (4 oz.) HERSHEY'S Unsweetened Chocolate Premium Baking Bar, broken into pieces

2 cups miniature marshmallows

1 cup MOUNDS Sweetened Coconut Flakes

1 cup coarsely chopped pecans

1 package (4 oz.) HERSHEY'S SPECIAL DARK Chocolate Premium Baking Bar, broken into pieces

1 tablespoon shortening (do not use butter, margarine, spread or oil)

1. Heat oven to 350°F. Combine pretzels and melted butter in small bowl; press evenly onto bottom of ungreased 13×9-inch baking pan.

2. Place sweetened condensed milk and unsweetened chocolate in small microwave-safe bowl. Microwave at MEDIUM (50%) 1 to 1½ minutes or until mixture is melted and smooth when stirred; carefully pour over pretzel layer in pan. Top with marshmallows, coconut and pecans; press firmly down onto chocolate layer.

3. Bake 25 to 30 minutes or until lightly browned; cool completely in pan on wire rack.

4. Melt SPECIAL DARK chocolate and shortening in small microwave-safe bowl at MEDIUM 1 minute or until melted when stirred; drizzle over entire top. Cut into bars. Refrigerate 15 minutes or until glaze is set.

Makes 36 bars

Simply Special Brownies

1 package (4 oz.)
   HERSHEY'S SPECIAL
   DARK Chocolate
   Premium Baking Bar,
   broken into pieces

½ cup (1 stick) butter or
   margarine

2 eggs

1 teaspoon vanilla
   extract

¾ teaspoon powdered
   instant coffee

⅔ cup sugar

½ cup all-purpose flour

¼ teaspoon baking soda

¼ teaspoon salt

½ cup coarsely chopped
   nuts (optional)

1. Heat oven to 350°F. Grease 9-inch square baking pan.

2. Place chocolate and butter in medium microwave-safe bowl. Microwave at MEDIUM (50%) 1 minute; stir. If necessary, microwave an additional 15 seconds at a time, stirring after each heating, until chocolate is melted and mixture is smooth when stirred. Add eggs, vanilla and instant coffee, stirring until well blended. Stir in sugar, flour, baking soda and salt; blend completely. Stir in nuts, if desired. Spread batter in prepared pan.

3. Bake 25 to 30 minutes or until wooden pick inserted in center comes out almost clean. Cool completely in pan on wire rack. Cut into bars.

Makes 20 brownies

Chunky Macadamia Bars

¾ cup (1½ sticks) butter or margarine, softened

1 cup packed light brown sugar

½ cup granulated sugar

1 egg

1 teaspoon vanilla extract

2¼ cups all-purpose flour

1 teaspoon baking soda

1¾ cups (10-oz. pkg.) HERSHEY'S Mini KISSES BRAND Milk Chocolates, divided

¾ cup MAUNA LOA Macadamia Baking Pieces

VANILLA GLAZE (recipe follows)

1. Heat oven to 375°F.

2. Beat butter, brown sugar and granulated sugar in large bowl until fluffy. Add egg and vanilla; beat well. Add flour and baking soda; blend well. Stir in 1 cup chocolate pieces and nuts; press into ungreased 13×9×2-inch baking pan. Sprinkle with remaining ¾ cup chocolates.

3. Bake 22 to 25 minutes or until golden brown. Cool completely in pan on wire rack. Drizzle VANILLA GLAZE over top; allow to set. Cut into bars.

VANILLA GLAZE: Combine 1 cup powdered sugar, 2 tablespoons milk and ½ teaspoon vanilla extract in small bowl; stir until smooth. Makes ⅓ cup glaze.

Makes 24 bars

Raspberry and Chocolate Streusel Bars

2½ cups all-purpose flour

1 cup sugar

¾ cup finely chopped pecans

1 egg, beaten

1 cup (2 sticks) cold butter or margarine

1 jar (12 oz.) seedless red raspberry jam

1⅓ cups (8-oz. pkg.) HERSHEY'S Dark Chocolate Baking Pieces Filled with Raspberry Crème

1. Heat oven to 350°F. Grease 13×9×2-inch baking pan.

2. Stir together flour, sugar, pecans and egg in large bowl. Cut in butter with pastry blender or fork until mixture resembles coarse crumbs; set aside 1½ cups crumb mixture. Press remaining crumb mixture on bottom of prepared pan. Stir jam to soften; carefully spread over crumb mixture. Sprinkle with baking pieces. Crumble remaining crumb mixture evenly over top.

3. Bake 40 to 45 minutes or until lightly browned. Cool completely in pan on wire rack; cut into bars.

Makes 36 bars

S'mores Sandwich Bar Cookies

½ cup (1 stick) butter or margarine, softened

¾ cup sugar

1 egg

1 teaspoon vanilla extract

1⅓ cups all-purpose flour

¾ cup graham cracker crumbs

1 teaspoon baking powder

¼ teaspoon salt

1⅓ cups (8-oz. pkg.) HERSHEY'S Mini Milk Chocolate Bars or 5 HERSHEY'S Milk Chocolate Bars (1.55 oz. each)

3 cups miniature marshmallows

1. Heat oven to 350°F. Grease 8-inch square baking pan.

2. Beat butter and sugar until well blended in large bowl. Add egg and vanilla; beat well. Stir together flour, graham cracker crumbs, baking powder and salt; add to butter mixture, beating until blended. Press half of dough into prepared pan. Bake 15 minutes.

3. Sprinkle mini chocolate bars over baked layer or arrange unwrapped chocolate bars over baked layer, breaking as needed to fit. Sprinkle with marshmallows; scatter bits of remaining dough over marshmallows, forming top layer. Bake 10 to 15 minutes or just until lightly browned. Cool completely in pan on wire rack. Cut into bars.

Makes 16 bars

Quarterback Blitz Bars

1 cup (2 sticks) butter or margarine

2¼ cups graham cracker crumbs

⅓ cup HERSHEY'S Cocoa

3 tablespoons sugar

1 can (14 oz.) sweetened condensed milk

1 cup HERSHEY'S Mini KISSES BRAND Milk Chocolates

1 cup HEATH BITS 'O BRICKLE Toffee Bits

1 cup chopped walnuts

1 cup MOUNDS Sweetened Coconut Flakes

1. Heat oven to 350°F. Place butter in 13×9×2-inch baking pan; heat in oven until melted. Remove from oven.

2. Stir together graham cracker crumbs, cocoa and sugar; sprinkle over melted butter. Stir mixture until evenly coated; press evenly with spatula onto bottom of pan. Pour sweetened condensed milk evenly over crumb mixture. Sprinkle with chocolate pieces and toffee bits. Sprinkle nuts and coconut on top; press down firmly.

3. Bake 25 to 30 minutes or until lightly browned. Cool completely in pan on wire rack. Cover with foil; let stand at room temperature several hours. Cut into bars.

Makes about 36 bars

Oatmeal Toffee Bars

1 cup (2 sticks) butter or margarine, softened

1 cup packed light brown sugar

2 eggs

1 teaspoon vanilla extract

1½ cups all-purpose flour

1 teaspoon baking soda

½ teaspoon ground cinnamon

½ teaspoon salt

1⅓ cups (8-oz. pkg.) HEATH BITS 'O BRICKLE Toffee Bits, divided

3 cups quick-cooking or regular rolled oats

1. Heat oven to 350°F. Grease 13×9×2-inch baking pan.

2. Beat butter and brown sugar in large bowl until well blended. Add eggs and vanilla; beat well.

3. Stir together flour, baking soda, cinnamon and salt. Gradually add to butter mixture, beating until blended. Set aside ¼ cup toffee bits. Stir remaining toffee bits and oats into batter (batter will be stiff). Spread batter in prepared pan; sprinkle reserved ¼ cup toffee bits over surface.

4. Bake 25 minutes or until wooden pick inserted in center comes out clean. Cool completely in pan on wire rack. Cut into bars.

Makes 36 bars

Chocolate and Peanut Butter Filled Peanut Butter Blondies

¾ cup REESE'S Creamy Peanut Butter

¼ cup (½ stick) butter or margarine, softened

½ cup packed light brown sugar

¼ cup granulated sugar

1 egg

2 tablespoons milk

1 teaspoon vanilla extract

1 cup all-purpose flour

½ teaspoon baking soda

⅛ teaspoon salt

1⅓ cups (8-oz. pkg.) REESE'S Milk Chocolate Baking Pieces Filled with Peanut Butter Crème or REESE'S Peanut Butter Chips

1. Heat oven to 350°F. Grease 8- or 9-inch baking pan.

2. Beat peanut butter, butter, brown sugar and granulated sugar in large bowl until well blended. Add egg, milk and vanilla; beat well. Stir together flour, baking soda and salt; add to peanut butter mixture, beating until well blended.

3. Spread one half of batter in prepared pan. Sprinkle baking pieces over batter. Drop remaining batter by ½ teaspoons over mixture, covering baking pieces.

4. Bake 25 to 30 minutes or until lightly browned. Cool completely in pan on wire rack. Cut into bars.

Makes 16 bars

Chocolate Almond Macaroon Bars

2 cups chocolate wafer cookie crumbs

6 tablespoons butter or margarine, melted

6 tablespoons powdered sugar

1 can (14 oz.) sweetened condensed milk

3¾ cups (10-oz. pkg.) MOUNDS Sweetened Coconut Flakes

1 cup sliced almonds, toasted* (optional)

1 cup HERSHEY'S SPECIAL DARK Chocolate Chips or HERSHEY'S Semi-Sweet Chocolate Chips

¼ cup whipping cream

½ cup HERSHEY'S Premier White Chips

To toast almonds: Heat oven to 350°F. Spread almonds evenly on shallow baking sheet. Bake 5 to 8 minutes or until lightly browned.

1. Heat oven to 350°F. Grease 13×9×2-inch baking pan.

2. Combine crumbs, melted butter and sugar in large bowl. Firmly press crumb mixture on bottom of prepared pan. Stir together sweetened condensed milk, coconut and almonds in large bowl, mixing well. Carefully drop mixture by spoonfuls over crust; spread evenly.

3. Bake 20 to 25 minutes or until coconut edges just begin to brown. Cool.

4. Place chocolate chips and whipping cream in medium microwave-safe bowl. Microwave at MEDIUM (50%) 1 minute; stir. If necessary, microwave at MEDIUM an additional 15 seconds at a time, stirring after each heating, until chips are melted and mixture is smooth when stirred. Cool until slightly thickened; spread over cooled bars. Sprinkle top with white chips. Cover; refrigerate several hours or until thoroughly chilled. Cut into bars. Refrigerate leftovers.

Makes about 36 bars

California Chocolate Bars

6 tablespoons butter or margarine, softened

½ cup granulated sugar

¼ cup packed light brown sugar

1 egg

1 teaspoon freshly grated orange peel

1 teaspoon vanilla extract

1 cup all-purpose flour

½ teaspoon baking soda

¼ teaspoon salt

½ cup chopped dried apricots

½ cup coarsely chopped walnuts

1 cup HERSHEY'S Mini KISSES BRAND Chocolates

MILK CHOCOLATE GLAZE, optional (recipe follows)

1. Heat oven to 350°F. Grease 9-inch square baking pan.

2. Beat butter, granulated sugar, brown sugar and egg in large bowl until fluffy. Add orange peel and vanilla; beat until blended. Stir together flour, baking soda and salt; add to orange mixture. Stir in apricots, walnuts and chocolates; spread in prepared pan.

3. Bake 25 to 30 minutes or until lightly browned and bars begin to pull away from sides of pan. Cool completely in pan on wire rack. Prepare MILK CHOCOLATE GLAZE, if desired; drizzle over top. Allow to set; cut into bars.

MILK CHOCOLATE GLAZE: Place ¼ cup HERSHEY'S Mini KISSES BRAND Milk Chocolates and ¾ teaspoon shortening (do not use butter, margarine, spread or oil) in small microwave-safe bowl. Microwave at MEDIUM (50%) 45 seconds or until chocolates are melted and mixture is smooth when stirred.

Makes about 16 bars

Cocoa Coconut Brownies

½ cup (1 stick) butter or margarine, melted

1 cup sugar

1 teaspoon vanilla extract

2 eggs

½ cup all-purpose flour

⅓ cup HERSHEY'S Cocoa

¼ teaspoon baking powder

¼ teaspoon salt

1 cup MOUNDS Sweetened Coconut Flakes, divided

1. Heat oven to 350°F. Grease 8-inch square baking pan.

2. Stir together butter, sugar and vanilla in medium bowl. Add eggs; beat well with spoon. Stir together flour, cocoa, baking powder and salt; gradually add to egg mixture, beating until well blended. Stir in ¾ cup coconut. Spread batter evenly in prepared pan. Sprinkle remaining ¼ cup coconut over top.

3. Bake 25 to 30 minutes or until brownies begin to pull away from sides of pan. Cool completely in pan on wire rack. Cut into squares.

Makes about 16 brownies

Peanut Butter Glazed Chocolate Bars

¾ cup (1½ sticks) butter or margarine

½ cup HERSHEY'S Cocoa

1½ cups sugar

1½ teaspoons vanilla extract

3 eggs

1¼ cups all-purpose flour

¼ teaspoon baking powder

PEANUT BUTTER FILLING AND GLAZE (recipe follows)

CHOCOLATE DRIZZLE (recipe follows)

1. Heat oven to 350°F. Line 15½×10½×1-inch jelly-roll pan with foil; grease foil.

2. Melt butter in medium saucepan over low heat. Add cocoa; stir constantly until smooth. Remove from heat; stir in sugar and vanilla. Beat in eggs, one at a time, until well combined. Stir in flour and baking powder. Spread batter evenly in prepared pan.

3. Bake 14 to 16 minutes or until top springs back when touched lightly in center. Remove from oven; cool 2 minutes. Invert onto wire rack. Peel off foil; turn right side up on wire rack to cool completely.

4. Prepare PEANUT BUTTER FILLING AND GLAZE. Cut brownie in half; spread half of glaze evenly on one half. Top with second half; spread with remaining glaze. Cool until glaze is set. Prepare CHOCOLATE DRIZZLE; drizzle over glaze. After chocolate is set, cut into bars.

Makes about 40 bars

PEANUT BUTTER FILLING AND GLAZE: Combine ⅓ cup sugar and ⅓ cup water in small saucepan; cook over medium heat to boiling. Remove from heat; immediately add 1⅔ cups (10-oz. pkg.) REESE'S Peanut Butter Chips. Stir until melted. Cool slightly. Makes about 1⅓ cups glaze.

CHOCOLATE DRIZZLE: Place ⅓ cup HERSHEY'S SPECIAL DARK Chocolate Chips or HERSHEY'S Semi-Sweet Chocolate Chips and 1 teaspoon shortening (do not use butter, margarine, spread or oil) in small microwave-safe bowl. Microwave at MEDIUM (50%) 30 seconds to 1 minute or until chips are melted and mixture is smooth when stirred.

Layered Cookie Bars

¾ cup (1½ sticks) butter or margarine

1¾ cups vanilla wafer crumbs

6 tablespoons HERSHEY'S Cocoa

¼ cup sugar

1 can (14 oz.) sweetened condensed milk (not evaporated milk)

1 cup HERSHEY'S SPECIAL DARK Chocolate Chips or HERSHEY'S Semi-Sweet Chocolate Chips

¾ cup HEATH BITS 'O BRICKLE Toffee Bits

1 cup chopped walnuts

1. Heat oven to 350°F. Melt butter in 13×9×2-inch baking pan in oven. Combine crumbs, cocoa and sugar; sprinkle over butter.

2. Pour sweetened condensed milk evenly on top of crumbs. Top with chocolate chips and toffee bits, then nuts; press down firmly.

3. Bake 25 to 30 minutes or until lightly browned. Cool completely in pan on wire rack. Chill, if desired. Cut into bars. Store covered at room temperature.

Makes about 36 bars

Double Chip Brownies

¾ cup HERSHEY'S Cocoa

½ teaspoon baking soda

⅔ cup butter or margarine, melted and divided

½ cup boiling water

2 cups sugar

2 eggs

1⅓ cups all-purpose flour

1 teaspoon vanilla extract

¼ teaspoon salt

1 cups HERSHEY'S Milk Chocolate Chips

1 cup REESE'S Peanut Butter Chips

1. Heat oven to 350°F. Grease 13×9×2-inch baking pan.

2. Stir together cocoa and baking soda in large bowl; stir in ⅓ cup butter. Add boiling water; stir until mixture thickens. Stir in sugar, eggs and remaining ⅓ cup butter; stir until smooth. Add flour, vanilla and salt; blend completely. Stir in milk chocolate chips and peanut butter chips. Spread in prepared pan.

3. Bake 35 to 40 minutes or until brownies begin to pull away from sides of pan. Cool completely in pan on wire rack. Cut into squares.

Makes about 36 brownies

INDEX

C

Cakes & Cheesecakes

Candy